Complete
Tai Chi Chuan

COMPLETE TAI CHI CHUAN

Dan Docherty

The Crowood Press

First Published in 1997 by
The Crowood Press Ltd
Ramsbury, Marlborough
Wiltshire SN8 2HR

www.crowood.com

This impression 2011

British Library Cataloguing in Publication Data

A catalogue record for this book is available from the British Library.

ISBN 978 1 86126 033 8

Typeset by Multimedia Works Ltd., Gloucester
Printed and bound in Spain by GraphyCems

Contents

Foreword
by Ilpo Jalamo

It gives me great pleasure to write a foreword to Mr Docherty's new book *Complete Tai Chi Chuan*.

I first met Mr Docherty in 1989 when I organized a seminar for my karate students in Finland to introduce them to Tai Chi Chuan. In that seminar, and in many others that followed, Mr Docherty's unique way of approaching this old Chinese martial art not only proved the practicality of the movements, but also the deep philosophy behind them.

Mr Docherty has the rare ability to explain Chinese theories in a way which is understandable to a western mind, and then to demonstrate the theory in practice. This harmony of ideas and their practical application makes this book very useful not only to Tai Chi students but to the martial arts community in general.

Ilpo Jalamo,
6th Dan Yuishinkai Karate

Foreword
by Cheng Kam

My name is Cheng Kam. I was born in the year of the Metal Horse in the town of Lin Tan, in Yu Nan district, Guangdong province. Let me tell you how Dan Docherty and I have been Tai Chi brothers and friends since 1976.

In 1958 I came to Hong Kong to seek a living, and ran the New Kam Garden Restaurant in Taikoktsui. In 1970 I set up the Lunggang Countrymen's Association, and in 1973 was elected president for life. Though occupied with business affairs, in 1976 I began training in the Tai Chi Chuan of the famous Master Cheng Tin-hung who, to strengthen the ties between teacher and brothers, set up the Hong Kong Tai Chi Association. In 1979 I was invited to be a Tai Chi instructor by the Recreation and Sports Department and by the urban council. I also taught at the Mongkok Neighbourhood Association and Chen Ching Social Welfare Association. In 1981 I helped set up the Hong Kong International Martial Arts Association, while in 1982 I helped Sifu Cheng set up the Chinese Boxing Association.

In 1976 I became a Door Person of Sifu Cheng and thus Kung Fu brother to Tong Chi-kin and Cinnabar (Dan Docherty). Since then I have supported Tai Chi martial arts, and young and vigorous fighters Tong Chi-kin and Dan Docherty in Lei Tai (full contact fighting platform) competition where fists and feet decide who is higher and who lower. Tong and Dan, like Sifu Cheng and I, were born in the Horse year.

In the fourth month of 1980, Sifu Cheng Tin-hung was appointed leader of the Hong Kong team at the 5th South-East Asian International Chinese Martial Arts Lei Tai Championships in Malaysia. I, Cheng Kam, was assistant team leader. At the first fighting platform in Penang, after a ferocious battle, Tong Chi-kin's Malaysian opponent gave up. At the second venue in Ipoh, Tong beat the local champion from Chi Ke Chuan style. At the third platform in Seremban, Dan Docherty faced the huge Roy Pink of Five Ancestors Boxing who outweighed Dan by more than 100lb (45kg). Though kicked from the platform, Dan came back to knock out his opponent in the first round with a Tai Chi Running Thunder Punch. Dan's opponent was unconscious for more than five minutes.

At the final fighting platform in Kuala Lumpur, Tong Chi-kin beat Shum of Dragon style and became champion of the middleweight division by defeating the Malaysian champion. Dan faced Lohandran of Chi Ke Chuan who was

Malaysian heavyweight boxing champion and winner of the heavyweight division at the 4th South-East Asian International Chinese Martial Arts Lei Tai Championships in Singapore. Though outweighed by more than 30lb, Dan defeated his opponent and became champion of the superheavyweight division.

I had many good times and jokes with my Tai Chi brothers and our master Cheng Tin-hung during our time in Malaysia, especially in Seremban. In the years that have followed I have taken part in many demonstrations with Dan and my other Tai Chi brothers, and we have attended competitions together in Hong Kong and abroad. In 1990 during the 1st Chung Hua Cup in Taiwan we shared rooms and spent the night talking of heaven and of earth. Now Master Cheng has returned to China, Tong Chi-kin has moved to Guatemala and Dan is always travelling, but whenever we meet, we eat and drink and talk of old times.

It is a pleasure for me to be invited to write this foreword and to wish Dan's book every success.

Cheng Kam
Hon. President, Hong Kong
Tai Chi Association

Preface

This book has taken me longer to write than I had hoped. A major factor for this was that I kept coming across new material, especially in the field of Tai Chi Chuan history, and this forced me to re-examine material I had already looked at with the result that the historical section is extremely detailed. In trying to make it accurate I found that at several points I was contradicting my teacher's writings and my own pre-conceived ideas. However, my teacher encouraged me to go for accuracy rather than sycophancy, and I have done so.

Most Tai Chi Chuan practitioners approach the art in a non-martial way, and I respect that. However, the title of this book is *Complete Tai Chi Chuan*, so I feel it is my duty to my publishers and my readers to examine all aspects of the art. I have therefore included sections on ritual initiation, 'inside-the-door' training, the inner form, competitions and *Dim Mak* which are either not to be found in other Tai Chi Chuan books or are glossed over with a brief mention.

In a sense, Tai Chi Chuan is such a vast subject that no book about it can ever be truly complete; to address this weakness, I look forward to receiving comments and criticism from my Tai Chi Chuan friends and enemies, as I most assuredly will. This book can fairly be said to represent the refined essence (to use a Taoist term) of many experiences and interactions all over the world.

Acknowledgements

I would like to thank here some of the many good people in Europe and the Far East who have helped me in my quest, with apologies to any left out: Geert, Lionel, John, Steve and Rob for drawing to my attention certain books and articles (including some on the Internet); my Chinese teachers for their patience; Mak Lai-han for a vital photo, and my elder brother, Tsui Woon-kwong, for a vital book. The great calligraphy is the work of Ms D. Choy; Karl and Orsi gave me useful comments and suggestions. Thanks also to Hans for putting up with me in Hong Kong.

Dr Death in Dublin, and Ilpo in Turku with their extensive martial arts knowledge were most useful debating partners in the fields of history and of vital point attacks respectively, while elder brother Ian was helpful in discussing our master and his method. Thanks to Mr Ma, caretaker of the Golden Pavilion Temple in Bao Ji, for giving unrestricted access, and to members of the Chen clan for showing me as much as they did (though I doubt they will appreciate my conclusions). Lee Yim-ping was a great help in Hong Kong and China. I would also like to thank Madam Chu Wai-man and my old friend Cheng Kam for their many kindnesses.

I appreciate the many useful chats with my colleagues in the British Council for Chinese Martial Arts and at the Tai Chi Union for Great Britain. In particular Ronnie Robinson, editor of *Tai Chi Chuan* magazine, has been a source of interesting material. Membership of these bodies has brought stimulating contact with instructors in Europe, too. Thanks also to Paul Clifton of *Combat* magazine for his help and support.

I would especially like to thank my students from their many and various countries for their help and support over the years, and I hope they feel that the efforts I have made in producing this book go some way to repaying them. The subtlety of Chinese language and thought can seem impenetrable to the average Western reader, so I have tried to retain the flavour of the original Chinese texts which I have translated, while trying also to make them clear and a pleasure to read. You must judge for yourself to what extent I have succeeded.

It is customary to dedicate books, so let me dedicate this one to scholars whose writings subvert the laws; to knight-errants who use their martial prowess to overthrow restrictions; and finally to all my flexible friends.

Dan Docherty

1 This is Complete Tai Chi Chuan

Tai Chi Chuan (sometimes rendered *Taijiquan*) is a Chinese martial art and exercise method – and a great deal more besides; a fuller definition will be provided later. The object of this book is to present an overview of the art itself and of different approaches to it in both the Far East and the West.

There is now great interest in Tai Chi Chuan throughout the world, and there are many books available on the subject. However, most of these deal only with certain aspects of the art, or they deal with the art from the point of view of one particular style, or they are too basic for the advanced reader or too advanced for the beginner. Many books also suffer from being contradictory or unclear, particularly as regards the history, and how to put theory into practice.

There are now many different styles of Tai Chi Chuan, and even styles within styles, and we will examine the more important of these in turn to trace and discuss their evolution and development.

The majority of Tai Chi Chuan practitioners only practise a few aspects of the art, and in most cases are also only aware of a few, and this applies to Chinese and non-Chinese alike. Furthermore, despite claims to the contrary, no-one alive today is practising precisely the art that Yang Lu-chan brought with him to Beijing around 1852. Since that time, successive generations of teachers have added to, and just as often have subtracted from the art; moreover in many cases the additions have been as detrimental as the subtractions. Nevertheless we must accept that any art, if it is to thrive, must develop and change to fit the circumstances of the society in which it exists.

Our journey in search of Tai Chi Chuan will cover thousands of years of Chinese history and culture. In addition on our travels we will examine medicine, self defence, physiological alchemy, weaponry, philosophy, religion, competition methods, aesthetics, teaching methodology and ritual initiation. It is a journey that will take us all over China and the Far East; a quest for truth and order in a jungle of mystery, fraud and conflicting theories.

THE FIVE ASPECTS OF TAI CHI CHUAN

There are five aspects which together make up the traditional Tai Chi Chuan syllabus. Here they are set out briefly, but they will be discussed in more detail later. They should be seen as complementary and interdependent rather than as completely separate entities.

The Hand Form (*Tao Chuan*)

This is a series of set moves performed in a flowing manner (Fig 1). Most schools of Tai Chi Chuan practise a traditional long form of some kind which includes many combinations and repetitions of techniques. It can take half an hour or more to do the traditional long form, while it can take up to two years to finish learning the form. This has led many teachers, particularly those teaching in the West, to develop short forms which can be learned more easily as they contain fewer combinations and repetitions; some of these can take as little as three or four minutes to perform. The mainland Chinese government has introduced simplified forms, but most practitioners prefer to practise traditional Tai Chi Chuan in all its aspects, rather than a simplified version.

In most styles the form is practised slowly and in a relaxed manner to enhance the respiration and circulation and to relax body and mind. In addition such practice helps to improve co-ordination, posture and balance.

Pushing Hands (*Tui Shou*)

This term is something of a misnomer, as some of the drills which come under this heading are not restricted to pushing or to the use of the hands. In fact the term refers to partnered drills which are designed to improve qualities useful in self defence such as sensitivity, balance, footwork, distance, angle, timing and co-ordination, as well as how to disrupt an opponent's centre of gravity. The drills described can be formal or spontaneous. There are also various methods of competition pushing hands.

Fig 1   Sifu Chu Wai-man from Hong Kong demonstrating Parry and Punch.

Certain schools use pushing hands practice as a way of therapy and interaction, but this is a modern and largely Western development.

Self Defence (*San Shou*)

The term *San Shou* literally means 'scattering' or 'dispersing hands'. Many Tai Chi Chuan schools do not teach self defence, and in the schools that do teach it, the *San Shou* is seldom taught in a practical way, but consists of merely attempting to apply techniques against an opponent in exactly the same way that the techniques are executed in the form. Many Tai Chi techniques are not found in the form, and in any case it is the form which is based on self defence techniques rather than the other way round.

The footwork and body evasion methods trained in pushing hands are concomitant with the strategies elucidated in the Tai Chi Chuan classics in applying the self defence techniques. Certain conditioning methods are also advisable. Tai Chi Chuan is fundamentally a counter-attacking style using low kicks, strikes, grappling and throwing techniques.

Weapons

The three Tai Chi Chuan traditional weapon forms are *Dao* (sabre/broadsword), *Jian* (straight sword) and *Qiang* (spear), and they are normally taught after the student has gained a certain level of proficiency in the hand form, pushing hands and self defence. The techniques of the weapon forms can be applied in self defence using the same strategies and tactics as in the case of the unarmed self defence techniques. We will discuss other weapons later.

Fig 2   Sifu Ian Cameron demonstrating Tai Chi sword.

Internal Strength (*Nei Kung*)

Internal strength is part of what is known as 'inside the door training': in other words, it is not something that is taught in open classes, but only after the student has undergone a formal initiation ceremony. It consists of twenty-four exercises: twelve Yin and twelve Yang, and these exercises have therapeutic, meditative and self defence aspects. They are seldom taught now and not many of those who do teach them are able to explain their function properly. In many respects this is the most effective form of training for both health and self defence, certainly far more so than the form, although it is a much more demanding type of training.

Fig. 3   Sifu Cheng Kam demonstrating Nei Kung.

In recent years a number of Tai Chi *Qi Gong* methods have come out of China which borrow partly from the form and partly from soft exercise methods such as Eight Pieces of Brocade (*Baduanjin*) to make up a simple exercise regimen that can be learned easily by older people and the sick. They are less sophisticated than traditional Tai Chi Chuan, but are useful where a student has difficulties in, or no time to learn Tai Chi Chuan. Certain *Kung Gong* methods are inherently dangerous or can be dangerous if practised incorrectly, as we shall see, so quality tuition is most advisable in this field.

Auxiliary Training

In addition to these five aspects it is necessary to learn the philosophical and theoretical side of the art to make sense of certain of the training methods, and to derive maximum benefit from your practice. Furthermore, there are other drills and training methods which don't quite fit into any of the categories given above, in particular certain conditioning methods.

TAI CHI CHUAN FOR ALL?

While Tai Chi Chuan can be practised by people of all ages, they cannot and should not be expected to practise it in the same way, as the type and method of the training should vary according to the physical and mental capabilities of the student. As with any martial art, generally the younger you are when you start, the better. My own daughter has been training in Tai Chi Chuan since before she went to school; firstly some simple *Nei Kung* exercises, then spear and then sabre. Only after all this did I start to teach her the form.

Sick and retired people, however, are normally more interested in learning the form to improve their health; and most students fall somewhere between the extremes of childhood and old age. I generally teach students the pushing hands and the martial aspects together with the form right from the first class, as I believe that practice of each aspect improves the student's ability to perform the others.

Learning Tai Chi Chuan

The first requirement for learning Tai Chi Chuan is to establish your reasons for doing so: thus, if you wish to learn it in all its aspects, then your choice of teacher will be limited as there are few of such calibre in either the Far East or the West. If you wish to learn only for health purposes, then as long as the teacher can do the form competently, this is usually enough for him/her to impart some basic skill.

The other requirements are that you must watch, ask, listen, read, and above all, practise: watch your teacher and fellow students, watch other teachers and students. Using the criteria mentioned in the chapter on form, you can analyse the good and bad points of technique. There is a lot of truth in the old saying that 'if you don't practise for one day, you know it; if you don't practise for two days, your teacher knows it; and if you don't practise for three days, everybody knows it.'

It is important to ask questions: most students ask the wrong questions and are therefore often given unhelpful answers. Furthermore, many teachers don't like answering questions, maybe because they don't always know the answers.

While it is useful to read appropriate books on Chinese philosophy, if you want to be able to use what you have learned, there is no substitute for daily practice. In Tai Chi Chuan, as in life, there are many armchair experts: don't be one of them.

Students

The word 'student' has a Latin root, in the verb *studere* meaning 'to be eager' or 'diligent' and by extension 'to study'. A student may just be someone engaged in the study of a particular subject, or he/she may be someone devoted to learning. Study itself has suggestions of examining, analysing, thinking, interest and purpose – yet how many students of Tai Chi Chuan practise with this attitude?

In Chinese martial arts there are various classifications of student. First, we use a family structure where students are classified as older/younger brothers/sisters, depending on when they started learning from a particular teacher. By the same token, one of your teacher's fellow students would then be your elder or younger aunt or uncle.

A general term for students of a master is *Tu Di* meaning literally 'younger brothers who are followers'; more succinctly, we can call them apprentices. Students are then divided into inside- and outside-the-door students: 'Inside-the-door students' are normally referred to as *Men Ren* meaning 'Door People' or more properly 'disciples' because they have undergone a ritual ceremony with their teacher; this is called *Bai Shi*. In Tai Chi Chuan we undergo this ceremony prior to being taught *Nei Kung*. Traditionally, only after the student and teacher had known one another for six years would the teacher offer to teach the *Nei Kung*; nowadays the period of time involved is usually much shorter, although it is still long enough for student and teacher to get to know one another properly.

Some teachers expect almost blind obedience from their students. However, this is not a healthy attitude: of course the student should respect the teacher's greater experience and knowledge, but this does not require him to ape his/her every action and opinion. Then again, some students are looking for a guru to direct their every thought and action rather than a teacher. But again, this is a path which has its dangers for students and teachers both because it is as bad to question nothing as it is to question everything.

Many people affirm that the evolution from student to master takes ten, or fifteen, or twenty years – but they are all wrong because the measure is not in terms of time, but of ability. My teacher became a full time professional Tai Chi instructor at the age of nineteen after three years of full time tuition from Qi Min-xuan. Yet I know other Chinese teachers who have trained for twenty, thirty or even forty years who are at best mediocre.

Some say that Tai Chi Chuan is more difficult to use in self defence than is hard style martial arts. However, the system that I teach is easier to learn because the basic techniques are freer as well as more versatile. In particular the defensive techniques are more efficient and require less physical effort on the part of the student. Also, many martial arts are taught as if the opponent can only be from the same art or as if he is a complete simpleton. I do not teach in this way.

Powerful students are not the best, nor are intelligent students, nor talented ones: the first requirement is spirit. With unquenchable spirit it is possible to beat stronger and better opponents; with power, technique and intelligence as well, such a student has the potential to become a master. How to acquire spirit? With practice, serious practice.

A good student will observe the following criteria: he
1. practises;
2. looks and listens;
3. thinks, then asks;
4. is neither too harsh nor too soft with his training partners;
5. constantly seeks to learn both inside and outside the class;
6. trains and competes honestly.

Too many students spend time talking, rather than doing. Learn by watching and listening to others, not just the teacher, and learn to discriminate. And if in doubt, ask. It is a major weakness of many students that they don't ask questions, and that when they do, they ask the wrong ones, such as 'What if...?' or 'How do I get out of...?' No teacher can teach you everything, even if he or she wanted to, which many don't. However, by practising certain basic techniques which follow key principles, the student will not find it necessary to ask the wrong question so often.

If you know something, then be positive, show that you know it. If you don't know something, then admit that you don't and seek to find it out. When learning something new, analyse it in the light of what you already know, and in turn use new ideas and information to analyse your old knowledge.

There is no point in bigger and stronger students relying mainly on their strength against smaller opponents. On the other hand, if techniques are not executed properly, for example out of a misguided sense of gallantry towards a lady opponent, then that lady is given a false sense of security. Furthermore, it is a deplorable trait amongst certain male students to attempt to correct female students of the same, or even of greater experience than themselves. I once saw a male student of six months' experience attempt to correct (wrongly) a female student with three years' experience!

However, experienced and capable students do have a responsibility to advise and encourage beginners; for instance they must accept that they have no divine right always to defeat every beginner in pushing hands or fighting. It is not enough to turn up at a class once a week and expect the teacher to do everything for you: it is up to you to get the most out of your training in a class, and to work on your own training. This is not just a physical approach, but includes reading and analysing.

Training and teaching should be honest. If you feel you can beat someone in pushing hands, for example, then do it. I have no time for instructors I have met in places such as Taiwan who, wanting to impress Westerners with their skills and expecting to beat them merely because they have been training for a certain number of years, then get angry with foreigners who failed to play their part and allowed themselves to be thrown around. In their way, teachers must be students too.

Discipline and Etiquette

In the Far East it is customary to address the teacher as *Sifu* and to address fellow students as elder/younger brother/sister depending on whether they learned before or after you. In my own classes, students call me Dan or (rarely) Mr Docherty. Some teachers require bowing both before and after each class, and also when students take a partner for pushing hands or self defence. My teacher only required a student to bow to him and more senior members of the school when undergoing *Bai Shi*, and I much prefer this approach; in other schools they seem to spend almost as much time bowing to one another as they do training.

Discipline and etiquette in Tai Chi classes are thorny questions. If too harsh and rigid, then the students live in fear of the teacher – though some martial arts students occasionally need to be hurt by the teacher, particularly when they are training in a way that is dangerous to themselves or to others. Some need strongly worded criticism from time to time; others require gentle encouragement – but they should not be treated the same unless they are the same.

TEACHING TAI CHI CHUAN

Although much has been written about the deeds and idiosyncracies of famous Tai Chi Chuan masters and how to learn Tai Chi Chuan, it is a remarkable fact that

very little has been written about teaching the art. Teaching Tai Chi Chuan is not like teaching tennis or boxing, and many (most?) Tai Chi Chuan teachers – Chinese and non-Chinese alike – have teaching methodologies which would very quickly earn them the sack from an academic institution. A typical example is the practice of many teachers to rely on students merely copying their movements, and then moving on once the student can do the technique more or less correctly. There is seldom any explanation or correction, the emphasis being on monotonous repetition. The more perspicacious and physically gifted students are often able to reproduce the teacher's

Fig 4.

movements exactly, but many end up doing Tai Chi Chuan which has severe technical defects. Some teachers go to the other extreme, making minute corrections to each posture which the student has little, if any, hope of replicating in his or her private practice.

Many teachers will try to avoid exposing gaps in their knowledge and/or to keep control of their students, either by teaching very slowly, or 'stealing' techniques from books and videos, or making up explanations on the spot. However, not all are like this: there is also a tradition in Tai Chi Chuan of teachers referring those students who have absorbed all their own knowledge, to a more experienced or highly skilled practitioner for more advanced tuition. Indeed, practitioners of one style of Tai Chi Chuan will often approach a teacher from another style to learn some particular skill which has either been lost in their own art or which their own master is unwilling to teach them. For example, a few years ago some Tai Chi friends who practise Hao style approached me to learn *Nei Kung*. As they were sincere and honest people and genuinely trying to improve their standard and that of their students, I was happy to teach them.

Once a teacher has taken on a student, he will have to decide not just how to teach him, but what to teach him. I teach Seven Star Step pushing hands first as this is comparatively easy to learn and it gives the student confidence to be able to do something in his/her first class. I also teach self defence applications and form from the first class onwards, as I believe that this helps a student to progress faster. After he has learned the short form he can then learn the long form, sabre, and if I feel he is ready, the Yin set of *Nei Kung*. After this he can learn the sword, the Yang set of *Nei Kung*, the spear and the inner art.

Before Yang Lu-chan went to Beijing and his descendants and students popularized the practice of Tai Chi Chuan, the art was taught on a much more intimate basis – 'inside the door' to no more than a handful of disciples at any one time. The commercialization of the art from the beginning of the twentieth century onwards has meant that although more and more people are learning the art, they are learning less of it.

2 Philosophy, Religion and Tai Chi Chuan

In this chapter we will examine Chinese ideas of cosmology as well as three of the major thought systems of the Chinese and their influence on the development of Tai Chi Chuan. Many of the ideas are an intriguing blend of philosophy and religion developed over many centuries. Because of its rich cultural origins Tai Chi Chuan offers at once a way of relating to the world and other people through its theory and practice that seems more realistic and more attractive than the ways offered by organized religions and politicians.

THE BEGINNING: CHINESE COSMOLOGY

Before looking at the Tai Chi symbol and Yin Yang theory it is helpful to examine Chinese concepts of the universe. The basic Chinese cosmology, traced from c1000 BC and developed by succeeding philosophers and schools of philosophy, is as follows:

Tao (Way)
cannot be spoken of and has no name – (Lao Tzu Ch 1).

Wu (Nothing)
Something and nothing mutually gave birth to one another (Lao Tzu Ch 2) so we have Wu Chi yet Tai Chi; Wu Wei (not to act against Nature) is Tao and from it came

Hun Tun (Chaos)
which is also Tai Chi (Supreme Ultimate Pole), a potentiality containing form, *Qi* (energy/vapour) and substance.

Tai Yi (Supreme Change)
took place and produced

Tai Chu (Supreme Starting)
of form and shape which caused

Tai Shi (Supreme Beginning)
of *Qi* (breath/energy) and then

Tai Su (Supreme Emptiness)
which brought the formation of substance and was the origin of

Liang Yi (the two symbols)
known as Yin (passive, female) and Yang (active, male), the interaction of which produced

Wu Xing (Five Elements)
of Metal, Wood, Water, Fire, and Earth which produced the Ten Thousand Things, including

Humanity
which is composed of Yin and Yang.

The Yin governs the seven emotions which on death descend to earth to become a *Gui* or demon; Yang governs the internal alchemy of *Qi*, *Jing* and *Shen* which on death ascend to heaven to become a spirit or immortal.

Much of the theory and terminology of Tai Chi Chuan derives from these concepts and terms, and those who formed and developed the art would have been well versed in them. We will discuss many of these ideas in both this and subsequent chapters.

THE TAI CHI SYMBOL

The term 'Tai Chi' first appears in Chinese literature in Appendix III to the *I Ching* (*Book of Changes*). This book is used for divination, and dates back to the Zhou dynasty (c1027–221 BC). It states:

> Therefore the *I* (Changes) has *Tai Chi*,
> It gives birth to the Two Forms (Yin & Yang)

This reference dates the term '*Tai Chi*' to around 200 BC at the latest. Earlier than this, much earlier, there is considerable evidence of a wide variety of martial arts and hygienic exercise in Chinese society. Tai Chi Chuan at its best is a marriage of these three forces, the martial, the therapeutic and the philosophical. It is a very appealing art as it balances the physical and dynamic with the spiritual and intellectual.

The earliest records of a Tai Chi symbol date from about the tenth century AD round about the time Chen Duan, the famous Taoist philosopher, lived on Hua Shan. The original symbol for the concept of Tai Chi seems to have been a simple circle. This is logical, as once we have a circle there is an inside and an outside; what is enclosed and what is not; what is circular and what is not: there is Yin and Yang. The inspiration for the circle may have come from the sun or moon, or it may simply be the inside of the circle made by the Eight Trigrams when they are arranged as the Eight Directions. Over the years what was the symbol for *Liang Yi* (two forms, ie Yin and Yang) replaced the simple circle and became known as the Tai Chi symbol. There are eight variations of the Tai Chi symbol, only one of which is auspicious as a symbol for a Tai Chi

Fig 5   Eight variations of the Tai Chi symbol.

school: that is why it appears as the logo of my association.

The white (or sometimes red) is called Yang and symbolizes the light of the sun, the active, masculine principle; the black (or sometimes blue) is called Yin and represents darkness, the passive, feminine principle. The two small black and white dots represent Yin in the Yang and Yang in the Yin respectively, as each principle is considered to contain a minimal amount of the other which allows them to interact and change.

The anticlockwise Tai Chi symbols are identified with the destructive cycle of the five elements, ie contrary to the *Tao*, and so are absolutely not suitable as symbols for a Tai Chi school. It may be that Bruce Lee's choice of an anticlockwise Tai Chi for his *Jeet Kuen Do* method contributed to his misfortune. Most Tai Chi masters, including those in China, are not aware of any of this.

In the light of the above, let us now define the term Tai Chi Chuan/Taijiquan, and then try to discover how that term should be applied. *Chuan* literally means 'fist', and by extension 'martial art', so we are not dealing here with something that is purely a health method or merely a form of moving meditation.

Tai Chi, the Supreme Ultimate, is the idea that the *Tao* or 'Way' is governed by two interacting and complementary principles known respectively as Yin and Yang. Heaven is Supreme Yang and Earth is Supreme Yin, so we have rain from Heaven fertilizing the Earth which takes it into the soil and produces life. Humanity stands between them, trying to match its actions with theirs, rather than going against them. Yin and Yang each contain an element of the other, and when one goes to an extreme it reverts to the other.

Tai Chi Chuan is therefore a *chuan* governed by the changes of Yin and Yang. For martial purposes Yin is soft or indirect, while Yang is hard or direct. Soft is not necessarily better than hard, or vice versa; it's a matter of using whatever is most appropriate under an existing set of circumstances. For example, we can use softness in the form of evasion and diversion to overcome hardness in the form of attacks, and we can use hardness to overcome softness by attacking the vulnerable points of the assailant's body. Beyond this, we need to be able to switch from Yin to Yang or Yang to Yin with ease. The same theory, as we shall see, also governs the health and technical aspects of the art.

The Changes of Yin and Yang

Appendix III to the *Book of Changes* goes on to say that:

> The Two Forms (Yin and Yang) give birth to the Four Emblems (Old Yin, Old Yang, Young Yin, Young Yang)
> The Four Emblems give birth to the Eight Trigrams (*Pa Kua/Ba Gua*)

> The Eight Trigrams determine good fortune and adversity;
> Good fortune and adversity give birth to the great business of life.

From the Eight Trigrams, through mathematical progression, we can eventually produce the sixty-four Hexagrams of the *Book of Changes*. Diagramatically this progression can be shown as depicted in Fig 6.

THE THREE DOCTRINES AND TAI CHI CHUAN

Some Tai Chi Chuan practitioners – mainly from the Chen style – say that there is

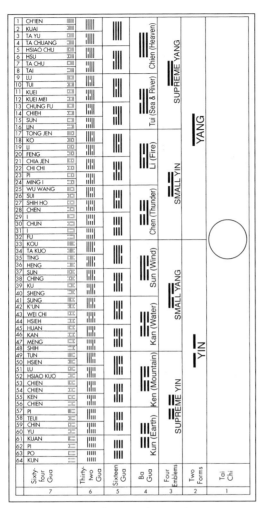

Fig 6   Changes of Yin and Yang from Tai Chi to the Eight Trigrams to the Sixty Four Hexagrams.

Buddhism are often called the three religions of the Chinese. 'Religions' is an overly simplistic translation of the Chinese character *Jiao*, which symbolizes a disciple under the instruction and discipline of a master. A more appropriate translation for this term would be 'doctrines/teachings', as Taoism, Confucianism and Buddhism in their various manifestations have philosophical and ethical aspects in addition to ritualistic and contemplative aspects. The three doctrines were not completely separate entities, but were very much interrelated. Let us examine each in turn to try to determine their influence on the development of Tai Chi Chuan.

TAOISM

It is often said that Tai Chi Chuan is a Taoist martial art. Taoism was, and is, two things: first it is a philosophy which emphasizes the importance of the *Tao* (Way) of harmony between humanity and the natural world. Second, it is a religion which combined these philosophical ideals with folk religion and later with certain Buddhist practices. The *I Ching* states:

> Establishing the *Tao* (Way) of Heaven, it
> is called Yin and Yang;
> Establishing the *Tao* of Earth, it is
> called Soft and Hard;
> Establishing the *Tao* of Man, it is called
> Benevolence and Righteousness.

There are many ideas current in Tai Chi Chuan which were derived from both religious, and even more so from philosophical Taoism. But what do we mean by *Tao* and Taoism? *Tao* is normally translated as the Way, but Chinese is often ambiguous and there are many Ways. Taoists were

no connection between Tai Chi Chuan and Taoism, and they are absolutely right: there is no connection between the Tai Chi Chuan *which they practise* and Taoism. I will explain this later in the section on Tai Chi Chuan history.

It is no easy task to decide where Chinese philosophy ends and religion begins. Taoism, Confucianism and therefore seekers of the Ways. These Ways were internal and/or external and included the practice of codes of ethics, hygienic exercise, meditation, internal alchemy of a sexual nature, rituals, spells, drugs and medicines. In Tai Chi Chuan all these elements are combined to a greater or lesser degree.

Many of the supposedly Taoist ways of exercise or ideas about medicine had little or nothing to do with either religious or philosophical Taoism, but instead were based on Chinese mythology or came from other sources. In addition the abstruse terminology used in Taoistic practices was occasionally taken literally, sometimes with harmful consequences. Religious and philosophical Taoist ideas influenced and were influenced in turn by Buddhism and the other schools of philosophy such as the Dialecticians.

Religious Taoism was divided into civil and martial ministries, and the latter included martial arts, and health and breathing exercises, all of which were necessary for exorcisms and other rituals.

TAI CHI CHUAN AND TAOISM

Let us look first at the philosopher, Lao Tzu (the Old Boy): in the *Tao Te Ching* (*Classic of the Way and Virtue*) he says:

'In focusing on *Qi* (vital energy), is it possible to become soft like a baby ?' (Ch X). This suggests that, well before 200 BC, training the breath as a relaxation method was already widespread. Many of the expressions and maxims of the *Tao Te Ching* are composed almost in the form of meditative chants – indeed, the same can be said of certain of the Tai Chi classics. Tai Chi Chuan uses a lot of the language as well as the ideas which appear in Lao

Tzu's work, not only in the practice of the hand form, but also and perhaps to a greater degree in the martial theory. For example, Lao Tzu talks about trying to attain emptiness and holding firmly to stillness, and says, 'Returning to the root is known as stillness' (Ch XVI). He also says:

'Crooked then complete, bent down then erect' (Ch XXII);

'Heavy is the root of light, stillness is the master of haste' (Ch XXVI);

'If you want to shrink something then you must stretch it; if you want to weaken something then you must strengthen it'(Ch XXXVI);

'*Tao* gives birth to One; One to Two; Two to Three; Three to the Ten Thousand Things; the Ten Thousand Things carry the Yin on their backs and embrace the Yang; through the mixing of their *Qi* (vital energy) they attain harmony' (Ch XLII)

The other great Taoist philosopher, Chuang Tzu, also makes a number of references to breathing, to motion being like water, to being attuned to changing with, rather than against, the *Tao*. Many of the more mystical ideas in Tai Chi Chuan are drawn from him. He was little interested in society in general, but mainly in the attainment of a personal *Tao* free from law, religion, family and the conventions of society. For example his allegory of personal salvation in the story of the giant bird called the Peng is referred to in the Tai Chi sabre form with the technique Peng Spreads its Wings.

Chuang Tzu also had a gift for mockery which he used against his peers such as Confucius, and even Lao Tzu. In response to Lao Tzu's idea of a great beginning to the cosmos, he stated that there must therefore have been a no-beginning and even a no-no-beginning. This concept of the great philosopher is with us in the idea of *Wu Chi* which is set out below.

In addition to the Taoism of the philosophers, there were also the many sects and cults of religious Taoism, some of which had imperial support at various stages in Chinese history. These were hierarchical and often bureaucratic. They blended their individual practices from ingredients which included shamanism, the occult, divination, prayer, ritual contemplation, martial arts, hygienic exercise and philosophy.

We can list the links between Taoism and Tai Chi Chuan as follows:

1. Ritual initiation of disciples is common to religious Taoism and Tai Chi Chuan.
2. In religious Taoism there is a strong emphasis on oral transmission of formulas/secrets from master to disciple. In the Tai Chi Chuan classic known as the *Song of the Thirteen Tactics* it is said, 'To enter the door and be led along the path, oral transmission is necessary.'
3. Chanting and recitation of mantras is common to both. In Tai Chi Chuan, the classics were chanted when training certain *Nei Kung* exercises.
4. In both Tai Chi Chuan and Taoism there is the concept of sending *Qi* (vital energy) to the *Tan Tien* (Cinnabar Field) below the navel to create *Jing* (vital essence), although some Taoists took this alchemical notion to an extreme. To increase this *Jing* to a maximum it is traditional for initiates in Tai Chi Chuan *Nei Kung* both to practise the exercises every day, and to abstain from all sexual practices for 100 days.
5. In Tai Chi Chuan, as in religious Taoism, there are ritual positions for the hands and fingers. In some Taoist rituals the index and middle fingers of the left hand point, while the little and ring fingers are bent in, as would be the case when using Tai Chi sword with the right hand.
6. In religious Taoism there are ritual stepping methods, such as the Step of Yu incorporating the Eight Trigrams. In Tai Chi Chuan there are likewise stepping methods and defence methods linked to the Eight Trigrams.
7. Tradition has it that Tai Chi Chuan was practised in the Taoist temples of Wudang Mountain, Bao Ji and the White Cloud Temple in Beijing. The Taoist sects on Wudang Mountain were renowned for martial practices, and indeed the mountain is named after Zhen Wu, the True Warrior.
8. Philosophical and religious Taoists and Tai Chi Chuan practitioners have a written tradition embodying theory and practice.

It may horrify some readers to realize that they are the inheritors not just of a deep and highly sophisticated philosophy, exercise system and martial art, but also the unwitting heirs of the religious and ritual aspects of Taoism. However, to ignore these aspects would be to close the door on the possibility of understanding the evolution of the art and what lies behind many of the concepts and practices.

CONFUCIANISM

Confucius (551–479 BC) aspired to be teacher to the gentleman/man of noble character, though any man could potentially be a gentleman. His curriculum of six classical books included the *I Ching*. He emphasized behaving in accordance with the principles of thinking of others (*Ren*), having respect for elders and social superiors (*Xiao*), and righteousness (*Yi*). Though often seen as a dry scholar, he advocated training in archery, charioteering and music as well as study for the aspiring gentleman.

TAI CHI CHUAN AND CONFUCIANISM

It was not just the Taoist who talked about the *Tao*, and as an aid to understanding the theory and philosophy of Tai Chi Chuan, it is helpful to read some Confucian texts such as the *Zhong Yong* (Doctrine of the Mean). This philosophical connection can be seen in the Tai Chi Chuan classics. For example, the Chinese philosophical terms *Lun* meaning discourse/analects and *Ching* meaning canon/classic, both appear as part of the title in, respectively, the *Tai Chi Chuan Lun* and the *Tai Chi Chuan Ching*. Furthermore the latter begins by quoting word for word from the Tai Chi Diagram Explanation (Fig 7) of the Neo-Confucian philosopher, Zhou Dun-yi.

There is a strong Confucian influence on Taoism and hence on Tai Chi Chuan. We can see this at work in the teacher/student relationship, which was traditionally very different from what we find in most Tai Chi Chuan classes in the West. For long periods in its history Tai Chi Chuan was taught by a master to a small intimate group of disciples who would spend much of their free time and sometimes all their time with the master, eating, sleeping, talking, drinking and learning.

The Tai Chi Chuan terms for disciple are *Men Ren* and *Di Zi*, both of which were also used to refer to the disciples of Confucius. *Men Ren*, or Door Person, is one who has entered the master's door, while *Di Zi* meant 'younger brother'; traditionally these terms would not be used until the student had undergone ritual initiation. Another term is *Tudi*, meaning 'younger brother apprentice'. The terms for 'teacher' or 'master' in Chinese martial arts is *Sifu/Shifu*. *Shi* meant 'teacher' or 'commander', while there were two characters for *Fu*, one of which meant 'tutor' while the other meant 'father'. Indeed, even today in the Far East the master is considered as the father of the martial arts family, while the students were elder and younger brothers and sisters in relationship to one another. This has led to a family structure where members considered duties and loyalties to the *Sifu* and family more important than to any others.

This family structure is reinforced by the conditions which the student accepts when undergoing ritual initiation to become a disciple. For more than two thousand years successive rulers of China have attempted to destroy such relationships: all have failed. At its worst, this system can produce criminal and political gangsters all the more powerful because they are sworn brothers united in a common cause, however pernicious. At its best, it can build a network of friendships and alliances all over the world.

EXPLANATION OF THE TAI CHI DIAGRAM

The 'Explanation of the Tai Chi Diagram' came from Chou Dun-yi (1017–73) who was the most outstanding representative of the Tai Chi Diagram Sect, one of three Neo-Confucian/Taoist sects which trace their origin from the great tenth-century philosopher Chen Duan from Hua Shan. It can be seen from the Diagram that Chou was concerned with Five Element theory as well as Yin Yang theory.

The Diagram is effectively a simplified version of the Chinese system of cosmogony which we looked at earlier. Starting from the top we have 'Wu Chi yet Tai Chi'. Tao and Tai Chi must come from that which is not Tao or Tai Chi – that is, Wu Chi: but if there is Wu Chi then there must also paradoxically be Tai Chi. We can see the concept of Wu Chi (No Pole/Ultimate) as being a Taoist one, and the concept of Tai Chi (Supreme Pole/Ultimate) as being Confucian. The Confucians sought order, both in the universe, in society and in the individual, so the idea of a fixed point such as the Pole Star as a centre from which order in the universe stemmed was very attractive. The Taoists were more concerned with change in harmony with the universe, so the idea that there was no one fixed pole, Wu Chi, but instead constant change, made perfect sense. The statement 'Wu Chi yet Tai Chi' reconciles these different approaches.

The philosophical concept of Wu Chi (or No Ultimate) predates Lao Tzu ie before the third century BC, and the idea of Tai Chi coming from Wu Chi is seen in the form where we move from the state of Wu Chi to Tai Chi (the Ready style), and then into Yin and Yang separating with the start of the form. Tai Chi Chuan can truly be said to be philosophy in action.

Below the empty Tai Chi circle we have the concentric half Yin, half Yang circles in which the Yang manifests itself in motion: when it reaches its limit it is followed by Yin which is manifest in stillness; in turn, when stillness has reached its limit there is a return to movement. In this way, movement and stillness, Yin and Yang in turn, each mutually becomes the source of the other. This is precisely what happens in Tai Chi form, in pushing hands and in self defence.

The interaction of Yin and Yang produces the Five Elements of Metal, Wood, Water, Fire and Earth. Water is largely Yin so is on the right, while Fire is largely Yang so is on the left. Wood produces Fire so is also on the left, while Metal produces Water (in the form of condensation) so is on the right. Earth is of mixed nature so is fixed in the centre. The crossed lines above Fire and Water show Yin generating Yang, and vice versa.

The Five Elements can operate in either a generative or in a destructive cycle. For example in the generative cycle Metal produces Water; Water produces Wood; Wood produces Fire; Fire produces Earth; Earth produces Metal. This is in accord with Nature and can also be represented by the clockwise-rotating Tai Chi symbol. In the destructive cycle Metal destroys Wood; Wood destroys Earth; Earth destroys Water; Water destroys Fire; Fire destroys Metal. This is contrary to Nature and can be represented by the anticlockwise-rotating Tai Chi symbol.

Using Yin Yang theory, each Element is stronger than two of the other Elements and weaker than the other two. Furthermore, each Element individually also has Yin and Yang aspects. Thus Metal could be sharp and shiny, or dull and rusty. Water could be a muddy pool or a mighty ocean.

The small circle below the Five Elements, and joined to them by four lines, again represents Wu Chi in which they are united.

The first large circle below the Five

Elements represents, on the left, the Tao of Chien, the trigram/hexagram for Heaven, which perfects maleness; on the right it represents the Tao of Kun, the trigram/hexagram for Earth, which perfects femaleness. The two Qi (energies) of maleness and femaleness interact and complement one another, bringing them back to the one Tai Chi (Supreme Pole).

The final circle represents the birth of the Ten Thousand Things caused by the interaction of the male and female principles and their return to the one Tai Chi (Supreme Pole). The techniques of Tai Chi Chuan can be seen in this way: beginning and ending at the same place.

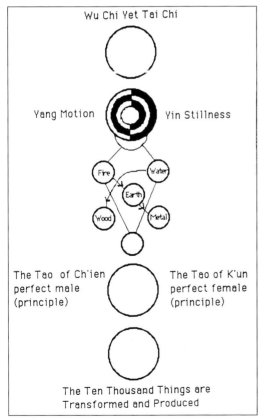

Fig 7.

BUDDHISM

Buddhism first entered China some time before 65 AD, and from that time there was a continuous contact and exchange of ideas; indeed, certain of the more esoteric aspects of tantric yoga were derived from Taoist internal alchemy techniques, and at a later date reintroduced to China when the original Taoist alchemy had almost died out.

BUDDHISM AND TAI CHI CHUAN

The most famous school of Chinese Buddhism is the Chan or meditation school, better known by its Japanese name of Zen. The first patriarch of the Chan school was the Indian monk Bodhidharma who introduced it to the Shaolin Temple in 527 AD. This was to be the most Chinese of all the Buddhist sects, and when I visited the Shaolin Temple in 1984 I found a number of Taoist symbols such as the Eight Trigrams and the Tai Chi, which is indicative of the interchange between these rival systems. Also many cryptic Chan allusions, such as the sound of one hand clapping, were borrowed from much earlier Chinese aphorisms such as 'A white horse is not a horse'. The success of Chan Buddhism led to the creation of the *Quan Zhen* (Complete Truth) Taoist sect, to which the founder of Tai Chi Chuan, Chang San-feng, belonged.

Some say that Chang San-feng was trained in martial arts in the Shaolin Temple, but this cannot be proven, and the terminology of Tai Chi Chuan, as we shall see, is heavily influenced by Taoism. The most famous centres of martial arts in China were to be found in Taoist and

Buddhist temples, and just as the various sects of these religions influenced one another, so did the various martial arts. So it is not surprising that many Tai Chi techniques, such as Drawing the Bow to Shoot an Arrow at the Tiger, and Planting the Fence, are intended as specific defences to traditional Shaolin attacks.

TAI CHI CHUAN AND MARTIAL PHILOSOPHIES

The theory elucidated in the Tai Chi Chuan classics, as well as the oral transmissions of the art, borrow extensively from military strategists such as Sun Tzu who wrote the *Art of War*. In the book Sun Tzu expounds on the use of philosophical principles such as Yin Yang theory to command an army and to wage war.

The Tai Chi Chuan theorists in turn have borrowed from the battlefield concepts such as 'retreat in order to advance', and references such as 'The mind is the commander, the *Qi* is the flag, the waist is the banner', and used them in the realm of personal combat and hygienic exercise. We will examine the classics in a separate chapter.

3 History of Tai Chi Chuan

Henry Ford remarked that 'History is bunk', and looking at some of the articles and books that masquerade as martial arts history, he may well have been right. History is important for Tai Chi practitioners as it tells us where we have come from, and from this we can hopefully deduce where we are now and where we should be trying to go in the future.

If we are to have history, we must have historians. As far as Tai Chi history is concerned, some have occasionally made real contributions while others have pushed the historical line that suits their own particular style or in some cases one that suits the Chinese Communist party; many of these articles and books are mere rehashings of what appears in earlier versions. Furthermore, in religious, political and martial history, many prefer a sanitized, uncomplicated version of complex events and personalities, rather than critical analysis and synthesis, and sometimes this preference for a pleasing version of events leads to a lack of tolerance towards those who attempt to argue a different version.

When something is widely believed or published, for many people it then becomes true, and believers in this 'truth' often seek to impose their beliefs on others. Mao Tse-tung said, 'No investigation, no right to speak', and 'Seek truth from facts'. Unfortunately, precious few people follow Mao's admirable advice – indeed, the Great Helmsman himself was not always noted for following these precepts. Many Tai Chi Chuan instructors are temperamentally incapable of admitting that there is something in their art or its history of which they know nothing, and are often incapable of accepting that another opinion may have some validity. When people with this outlook come to write history, it is indeed bunk.

In 1728, the Yong Zheng emperor issued an imperial prohibition on martial arts, condemning its instructors as 'drifters and idlers who refuse to work at their proper occupations, who gather with their disciples all day, leading to gambling, drinking and brawls'. However, more than two centuries later we look back on the same past as a golden age of great masters with high levels of ability and great virtue. Indeed we now have a deification of old masters. In the same way that Zhen Wu Shen, the True Martial God, became patriarch of certain cults during the Boxer Rebellion, so long dead masters are resurrected and their alleged opinions, deeds and abilities invoked to give credibility to those of modern practitioners.

What Style?

There exists now in both East and West a plethora of what purport to be different styles of Tai Chi Chuan. This situation raises two fundamental questions: what is a style? And is the style being practised Tai Chi Chuan?

The Chinese use four main terms to denote a style of martial arts. The first and most obvious is '*Chuan*', which literally means 'fist' as in 'Tai Chi Chuan'. But of course there is more than one type of Tai Chi Chuan.

The next term in common use is '*Jia*' or family, as in '*Sun Jia*' or Sun family. Those practising such a system are not always family members, but invariably believe themselves to be learning the secret transmission of the family in question.

The third term in common use is '*Shi*' which literally means 'work done after a model or pattern'. So, for example, '*Wu Shi*', meaning 'in the model of Wu' – but which Wu?

Finally the term '*Pai*' is used to denote a school or sect – and is often also used in connection with schools of philosophy or religious sects.

A style can be said to exist where a leading exponent of a particular martial art possesses certain unique features which set the art he practises apart from others. People began referring to Wu family/style Tai Chi Chuan and Yang family/style Tai Chi Chuan when they noticed

Fig 8　Sifus Bob Lowey and Ronnie Robinson practising Cheng Man-ching two person form.

differences in the teaching of Wu Jian-quan and Yang Cheng-fu who were con-temporaries. For example, in the Wu form there is only one Step Back to Beat The Tiger, while in the Yang there is one on the left, followed by one on the right. In the Yang form, Embrace Tiger and Return to Mountain follows Cross Hands, while in the Wu form this order is reversed. Also there are differences of posture, pushing hand drills and weapon forms.

As Tai Chi Chuan has become more widespread and variations have begun to emerge between different teachers, it has become common practice to divide Tai Chi Chuan into styles named after the famous masters of the past: Yang, Wu, Sun, Hao, Chen and so on. However, Chris Thomas who teaches Chen and Cheng Man-ching-style Tai Chi in Macclesfield, once remarked to me that only one person ever practised Cheng Man-ching-style Tai Chi Chuan, and that was Cheng Man-ching. And Chris is absolutely right: if the reader were to visit a hundred schools of Yang-style Tai Chi, he would find a hundred variations of this style, and from the writings of his students it is evident that Yang Cheng-fu changed his style at least three times.

The same applies to the other Tai Chi 'families'. For example in 1980, the Wu family published *Wu Family Tai Chi Chuan* in Hong Kong (this book will be discussed again later). The book featured Wu Jian-quan and his son, Wu Gung-yi, performing hand form. The techniques bore the same name, but were executed in a quite different way, the father's deep stances and extended movement contrast-ing with the son's high stances and limit-ed extension. So who is doing true Yang style? Who is doing true Wu style? Most Tai Chi instructors accept the principles

elucidated in the Tai Chi Chuan classics, even if in some cases they are not quite sure what these are. It is then only a ques-tion of whether they are capable of prac-tising these principles effectively or not.

Using the term 'Tai Chi' does not auto-matically confer legitimacy. For example a group in Britain practises Tai Chi Ribbon and Tai Chi Dance and claims to be the oldest style of Tai Chi Chuan, with a history of more than 2,000 years. They also claim to be able to move people with-out touching them. The question is not whether regular Tai Chi instructors believe all this (without exception they do not), but whether or not members of this group themselves truly believe that they

Fig 9   Temple buildings on the Southern cliff of Wudang Mountain.

are practising Tai Chi Chuan. For a style to be called Tai Chi Chuan it is not enough that it contains slow and relaxed movements; you could conceivably teach karate or Wing Chun in this way, and some people are actually doing this very thing. There must be a lineage; there must be a clear connection between what is being practised and the Tai Chi Chuan classics.

There are two major theories as to the origins of Tai Chi Chuan: one suggests that Tai Chi Chuan originated on Wudang Mountain with the Taoist, Chang San-feng. The other theory suggests that the art originated in the Chen family village.

Fig 11 Drawing by Jane Tucker: the entrance to the Chen family village.

THE STARTING POINT

There are many discrepancies in both what the Chen clan and the Yang lineage systems say: in fact, their claims are at a variance on almost every major issue, although there is little attempt at analysis in most books. What I wish to do is to state first of all what we are certain about, then to examine the other evidence in a forensic manner.

We are now entering a minefield situated in a maze. With Chinese language there are many dialects and regional variations in pronunciation which can lead to misunderstandings between individuals from different localities. Many characters sound the same as others though written

Fig 10 Stone stele of Chang San-feng on Wudang Mountain.

differently, or though sounding different are written in a very similar manner to one or more other characters with quite different meanings. Literati would often change their names to more auspicious ones, or have a pen name. For example, although my teacher was born Cheng Ngar-man, he is widely known as Cheng Tin-hung. Also many members of the literati would have nicknames identifying them with a particular place or activity.

There are also problems with dates and dating. Not until well into the twentieth century did Chinese adopt the Western method of dating in terms of AD and BC, and the months starting in January and ending in December. It was customary to

refer to the dynasty and the particular year of the reign name of the emperor, and then which day of which lunar month of that year. During the dynasties which preceded the Ming, it was common to have emperors change their reign name every few years. Needless to say, this has led to much confusion regarding names and dates. In Tai Chi history there are possibly two Chang San-fengs who lived at different times; a Wang Zong who may also have been called Wang Zong-yue, and yet another Wang Zong-yue; and there are two Chen Wang-tings.

Finally, much of what is now written about Tai Chi history was originally part of an oral transmission and therefore cannot be checked by reference to written records.

It was with the arrival in Beijing of Yang Lu-chan in 1852 that Tai Chi Chuan became well known, and most Tai Chi Chuan practised today came from Yang, directly or indirectly. So let us start with him.

Yang Lu-chan

Also known as Yang Fu-gui, he was born in the city of Guangping in Yongnian County, Hebei province, traditionally in the year 1799. We know that in his youth he went to the Chen family village in Henan province where he learned Tai Chi Chuan from Chen Chang-xing. He returned to Guangping and then went to Beijing.

Why did he leave his home? Why go to the remote Chen village? Why return home to Guangping? Why go to Beijing? Why, if the Chen family are truly the founders of Tai Chi Chuan, did they teach an outsider like Yang Lu-chan so well that he was known as Yang Wu Di (Yang the

Fig 12   The author in one of the courtyards in the Forbidden City.

Fig 14   Hut at the rear of Chen De-hu's villa, where Yang Lu-chan is said to have lived.

Fig 13 Statue of Chen Chang-xing passing the secrets of Tai Chi Chuan to Yang Lu-chan.

Invincible), became combat instructor to the Manchu Bannermen and teacher to the brother of the Ching emperor? The Chen village is small and remote even today, so how much more it must have been when Wu Tu-nan, the Tai Chi Chuan historian, visited it in 1917 – and more so still when Yang arrived there a century before Wu. There are numerous variations on the theme of how Yang arrived at the village and learned Tai Chi Chuan. One suggests that one of the Chen clan recruited him as an indentured servant when he was about ten years of age – this would have been around 1810 – and that while working as such in the house where Chen Chang-xing taught, he learned Tai Chi Chuan surreptitiously.

Another theory is that as a young adult Yang had heard of Tai Chi Chuan being practised at the village, had therefore left his home in Hebei province perhaps around 1820 with the express intent of learning the art at the village, and that naturally he sought some employment there. Stories about him working as a servant and learning the art secretly are typical of the later embellishments which are to be found in the biographies and stories about Chinese (and non-Chinese heroes) throughout the ages. As to why an outsider should have been taught so well, this requires a detailed examination of the claims of the Chen clan in relation to the founding of Tai Chi Chuan, and how it came to their village.

Whom did Yang teach? Firstly he taught his sons. The first son, Feng-hou (1835–81) is hardly mentioned in most books, and I can find no record of him accompanying his two younger brothers and his father to Beijing. Where Feng-hou is mentioned, it is to say that he had no students as he died young – yet he seems to have survived his father by almost ten years and lived into his forties! The second son was Ban-hou (also known as Yang Yu, 1837–92), also known as 'Invincible Yang'; some books have him teaching people before his father went to Beijing, when he would have been less than fifteen years old according to the dates which we have for him. The third son, Jian-hou (or Yang Jian, 1839–1917), also received the art.

Yang must have been more than just a fighter, as one of his students was the brother of the Ching emperor himself. It is said that because of this, his other personal students had to go through the *Bai Shi* ceremony with Yang Ban-hou as they could not be the Tai Chi brothers of a member of the royal family.

Most authorities give 1852 as the year of Yang Lu-chan's arrival in Beijing, when he was perhaps fifty-three years old. This was only one year before the death of his master Chen Chang-xing, and late in life to start to make a reputation as a martial arts master. Furthermore Yang's sons were born from 1835–39, that is, when Yang is supposed to have been in his late thirties: this is also late in life by the standards of the time. Two other students of Chen Chang-xing were already in Beijing before Yang got there: Li Bo-gui (who is said to have accompanied Yang when he first went to the Chen village) who worked as an armed escort for merchants; and Chen Long – so here we have a connection between Tai Chi Chuan and Beijing before Yang went there.

Around 1850, Lu-chan returned home to Guangping in Yongnian county where he taught Wu Yu-xiang and his two brothers who trained with him, although we don't know for how long or in what detail. If any of these earlier students went through *Bai Shi* with Yang Lu-chan, they would be Tai Chi elder brothers of the Emperor's brother! Until recently, Wu was the only one of Yang Lu-chan's students known as a writer on Tai Chi Chuan, although he had no particular reputation as a fighter – unlike Wang Lan-ting, Ling Shan, Quan You and Wan Chun, who were all members of the Imperial Guard, known to be effective fighters, and who conversely had no reputation as writers on the art.

Of Yang Lu-chan's students, apart from his sons, only Wu Yu-xiang, Quan You, Ling Shan and Wang Lan-ting seem to have actually taught anybody. In every way Yang Lu-chan is the pivotal figure.

THE CHEN FAMILY VILLAGE

The trail takes us back now to the Chen family village, Chenjiagou, because we know that Yang Lu-chan learned Tai Chi Chuan there from Chen Chang-xing.

Geography of the Chen Village

It is instructive to look at the geography of the Chen village. As we enter it down a long dusty road, the cemetery is on the right, and thirty yards down the road from the cemetery, on our left is the high wall which surrounds Chen De-hu's house, where behind the thick wooden doors Chen Chang-xing taught Tai Chi Chuan to Yang Lu-chan and others. Three hundred yards or so further on we come to the end of the village road and find ourselves at the entrance to the grounds of the Chen training hall which is of modern construction. Training in the Chen-style *Pao Chui* method still goes on in the large open area outside the hall.

GEOGRAPHY OF THE CHEN FAMILY VILLAGE

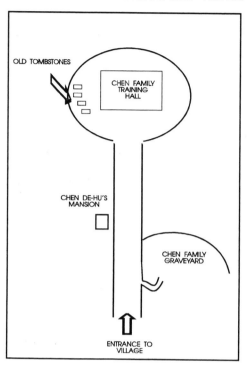

Fig. 15. Map of the Chen village.

Fig 16 Entrance to Chen De-hu's villa.

Tai Chi Chuan and the Chen Family Village

Did Chen Chang-xing learn Tai Chi Chuan from another member of the Chen clan or from an outsider? Let us examine the Tai Chi Chuan practised by the Yang Lu-chan lineage and compare it with the art now taught by the Chen clan. I use the phrase, 'now taught by the Chen clan' advisedly, because they claim that what Chen Chang-xing taught was the 'old two *Tao Lu* (forms) in big frame' and that this is what was handed down by his great-grandson Chen Fa-ke (1887–1957) to the present generation.

Yang Lu-chan died in 1872. We cannot be certain in every detail about the form or forms which he taught, but we can compare forms taught by those who follow him in the lineage. Although there are a few variations in the sequence, and sometimes slightly different names are used for the same techniques in the long forms practised by my teacher's school, the Wu Jian-chuan school, the Yang Cheng-fu school and the Wu Yu-xiang, the sequence itself and the names of the techniques are largely uniform. The way of moving is also largely the same, being fluid, with few sudden movements. In all these styles the long form is performed slowly. This is even the case in the form which Wu Yu-xiang developed, based on his training with Yang Lu-chan and one month's instruction from Chen Qing-ping at the Zhao Bao village.

So what of the Chen style? There are supposedly two major variations of this art. One is that handed down by Chen Qing-ping in the Zhao Bao village called 'new style' and 'small frame' (high stances, minimal movement). The other, 'old style' and 'big frame' (long stances, extended technique), is that taught in the Chen village which the Chen clan say was brought to Beijing in 1929 by Chen Fa-ke. Let us deal firstly with the art taught in the village today.

The Chens claim that around 1650 after the overthrow of the Ming dynasty, their ninth generation ancestor, Chen Wang-ting, handed down five *Lu* or routines of Tai Chi Chuan, one *Lu* of *Pao Chui* (Cannon Punch) and one routine of 108 technique Long Boxing. By the time of the fourteenth generation, Chen Chang-xing (1771–1853) was only able to hand down two 'old *Tao Lu*' in 'big frame', ie the *Pao Chui* form and a Tai Chi form.

So what happened? Why did five out of seven forms disappear? Were either of the two forms which the Chens say Chen Chang-xing taught, the same as the long form which we have in Yang lineage systems, or the same as either of the two remaining forms now practised in the Chen village? Some commentators such as Wu Tu-nan have stated that the forms now practised in the village were revised by Chen Fa-ke. The long forms practised by Yang Lu-chan lineage styles are fairly uniform in terms of names of techniques, sequence and method of performance. Let us now compare these forms with those practised in the Chen family village.

First of all let us compare names. Yang lineage techniques, such as Single Whip, Cloud Hands, Pat the Horse High and Fair Lady Works at Shuttle, all occur in both the Chen village Tai Chi Chuan and *Pao Chui* forms. The Chen Tai Chi form also includes White Crane Spreads Its Wings, Brush Knee Twist Step, Fist Under Elbow, Fan Through the Back, Wild Horse Parting Mane, Golden Cockerel on One Leg, Lotus Leg, Punch the Groin, Ride the Tiger and Tai Chi in Unity. The *Pao Chui* form also

includes Parry and Punch, and White Snake Puts out Its Tongue. There are also a few other techniques where there is a degree of similarity in the names between the Chen forms and names of techniques in the other forms.

Having identified certain similarities in the names of techniques, let us now look at differences. Techniques such as Flying Oblique, Raise Hands Step Up, Stroking the Lute, Separate the Legs, Box the Ears, Snake Creeps Down and Slap the Face and the inner form techniques, amongst others, cannot be found in the Chen forms.

Chen Tai Chi form techniques such as Buddha's Warrior Attendant Pounding Mortar, First Conclusion, Hidden Hand Punch, Bend Back and Use Shoulder, Blue Dragon Flies Up From The Water, Three Palm Changes, Retreat and Press Elbow, Rub the Foot, Hit Ground With Fist, Animal Head Posture, Hurricane Kick, Small Grasp and Hit, Double Shake Foot, White Ape Offers Fruit, Sparrow Ground Dragon and Face Opponent Cannon, do not occur in the Yang Lu-chan lineage long forms.

In the Chen *Pao Chui* form, techniques which do not appear in the Yang Lu-chan lineage include Buddha's Warrior Attendant Pounding Mortar, Guard The Heart Punch, Attack Waist Press Elbow Punch, Wind Blowing Plum Blossoms, Hidden Body Punch, Turning Flowers Dancing Sleeves, Hidden Hand Punch, Continuous Cannon, Retreat Riding Unicorn, Firecracker on Left and Right, Animal Head Posture, Fist Colours Eyebrow Red, Yellow Dragon Leaves Water, Sweep Ground With Leg, Rush On Left and Right, Four Head Cannon and many others.

Why do the Chen village forms contain

many techniques not found in the Yang Lu-chan lineage forms, and vice versa? Where do the techniques peculiar to the Chen village forms come from? Where do the techniques peculiar to the Yang Lu-chan lineage come from? Where do the techniques that do have the same name in both lineages come from?

In the syllabus of the Chen school there are the Tai Chi *Tao Lu* and the *Pao Chui Tao Lu*. The *Kung* training is in the forms which emphasize twisting and vibrating to create Reeling Silk Energy (these forms can be old or new and small or big frame); there are also applications for the techniques, but these are not taught at first.

There are five types of pushing hands, although according to Chen stylist, Feng Zhi-qiang, in 'Chen-style Taijiquan', these do not follow the Thirteen Tactics of Tai Chi Chuan nor do they follow a fixed pattern – indeed, many Tai Chi stylists would consider Feng to be violating a number of fundamental Tai Chi principles in his demonstration of Chen-style pushing hands in the book.

Chen weapons include single sabre, double sabre, single sword, double sword, double mace, pear blossom spear, white ape staff, spring and autumn halberd (in different weights) and 'Sticking Spears' training. In addition they practise some *Qi Gong* for health.

The Yang Lu-chan lineage syllabus has eight major methods of pushing hands and many variations; there are twenty-four Yin and Yang *Nei Kung* exercises, and forty-eight major *San Shou* fighting techniques, including Five Element Arm, Running Thunder Hand, and Flying Flower Palm which are not named in any hand form. The sword, sabre and spear forms and techniques are radically different from those of the Chen style.

Finally the Yang lineage systems have many other concepts and writings to which the Chens do not subscribe.

Chen Style and the Chuan Jing

According to Tang Hao, Tai Chi historian and student of Chen Fa-ke, twenty-nine of the thirty-two techniques of the *Chuan Jing* (*Classic of Boxing*), are to be found in the Chen style. The *Chuan Jing* was written by General Qi Ji-guang (1528–87) of the Ming dynasty, and represents a synthesis of sixteen different schools of boxing.

Of the thirty-two techniques of the *Chuan Jing*, I have identified nine which bear the same or a similar name to an existing Tai Chi Chuan technique of the Yang Lu-chan lineage styles. For example the second technique of the *Chuan Jing* is Golden Cockerel Stands on One Leg, and it bears a strong resemblance to the Tai Chi technique of this name. Likewise the third technique, Pat the Horse, is similar to Tai Chi's Pat the Horse High. However, more than twenty techniques of the *Chuan Jing* do not resemble Yang lineage techniques, either in their names or in the illustrations or descriptions shown.

It is possible that Tai Chi Chuan, or an art from which it was derived, was the source of techniques in the *Chuan Jing* which bear a resemblance to Tai Chi Chuan techniques. Conversely it is possible that some Tai Chi Chuan techniques were copied from, or altered to look more like, similarly named techniques in the *Chuan Jing*, or that names of techniques given in the *Chuan Jing* were adopted. Because of the dearth of reliable written sources we have yet another mystery. In the long history of Chinese martial arts and in particular Tai Chi Chuan, perhaps as much has been forgotten or lost as has been remembered.

The Chens suggest that the Yangs (Gu Liu-xin says Yang Lu-chan's sons) changed the Chen old-style Tai Chi Chuan and *Pao Chui* forms which Chen Chang-xing taught them. Another possibility is that one of the Chen clan blended in almost all of the techniques from the *Chuan Jing* with the *Pao Chu*i method which had existed in the Chen family for generations, and that quite separately Tai Chi Chuan influenced and was influenced by other styles so the names of some tech-niques are similar to some from the *Chuan Jing*. If the Chens did adopt *Chuan Jing* techniques, it is likely that Chen Wang-ting is responsible, as the Chens claim that around 1650, sixty to seventy years after the publication of the *Chuan Jing*, he created a new system of boxing.

If Yang lineage techniques come from the Chen family art, why do only some have a connection with the *Chuan Jing* while most do not, and why are none of the inner techniques of Yang lineage long forms, or the techniques of Tai Chi *Nei Kung* mentioned in the *Chuan Jing* or the Chen family art?

Chen Style and the Shaolin Temple

Not only are many Chen-style techniques – in particular the stamping and jumping – reminiscent of Shaolin methods, but some techniques (such as Buddhist's Warrior Attendant Pounding Mortar) are found in the Shaolin boxing methods which came from the Buddhist temple of that name at the foot of Mount Song. This and other Chen-style techniques come from a form said to have been invented by the first Tang emperor. It is natural that the martial art of the Chen family village

Fig 17　The author at the entrance to the Shaolin Temple.

should have been influenced by Shaolin methods as they are both in Henan province and only a few hours apart by road.

Chen Wang-ting

In a report dated 9 June 1980 in the third edition of the *Physical Education Newspaper*, Gu Liu-xin said that he had formerly wrongly believed that the Chen Wang-ting from the Chen village, who in 1640 had led rural militia to support the local magistrate in quelling an uprising, and the Chen Wang-ting from South Manchuria, who had been an imperial censor and received rewards from the emperor before his death in 1630, were one and the same, when in fact the *Ting* characters in the two names are different. He had published this view in two books. Only after the downfall of the Gang of Four was he able to correct his mistake.

Wu Tu-nan has related how in 1917 he

went to the Chen village and accompanied Chen Xin to the family graveyard; Chen Xin was the schoolmaster and later putative author (at least three other Chen clan members were involved in its publication) of *Chen Shi Taijiquan Tu Shuo*. There they saw Chen Wang-ting's tombstone on which it was written '*Wu Xiang Sheng*' meaning a military graduate at county level, the equivalent to a modern-day, elementary school graduate.

In October 1995 I was taken round the Chen village by Chen Zao-sen, a senior Chen style instructor. I found that all the old tombstones had been removed from the cemetery and now lay on the ground outside the *Pao Chui* training hall of the Chen clan. I can't say whether these were the original tombstones; in any event, none of them mentioned Tai Chi Chuan. Bright new tombstones had been erected in the cemetery, praising the Chen family ancestors and their contribution to Tai Chi Chuan. All the new monuments and tombstones were directed at honouring

Fig 19   The new gravestones in the Chen family cemetery.

Chen Wang-ting as the founder of Tai Chi Chuan. I did not see a single item of any antiquity which mentioned Tai Chi Chuan.

I asked about Chen Chang-xing's grave as I couldn't see it in the cemetery, and was told that there wasn't one. He is not honoured in any of the rooms in the Chen family *Pao Chui* training hall, and apart from his name on a new black tablet in the training hall giving the Chen family martial arts lineage, the only sign of him that I could find in the village was in a museum being created with Taiwanese money in the grounds of the house where he taught Tai Chi Chuan to Yang Lu-chan.

Outsiders and the Chen Family Village

Apart from Yang Lu-chan, at least two other outsiders are said to have had a strong influence on Tai Chi Chuan in the Chen family village: Wang Zong-yue and Jiang Fa. Gu Liu-xin in *Pao Chui – Second Form of Chen Style Tai Chi Chuan* credits

Fig 18   The old gravestones of the Chen family.

Wang Zong-yue from Shan You in Shanxi province with writing *The Tai Chi Chuan Treatise* (*Lun*), *The Song of the Thirteen Tactics* (*Shi San Shi Ge*) and *The Fighter's Song* (*Da Shou Ge*). The Yang lineage credit Jiang Fa as being the teacher of Chen Chang-xing.

The Chens claim to be the source for true Tai Chi Chuan, yet they accept that the outsider, Wang Zong-yue, wrote these major works, and many books on Chen Tai Chi include them. Furthermore, while Wang's writings are given great importance in all Yang Lu-chan lineage styles, none of these styles attaches any importance to the writings of members of the Chen clan, such as Chen Xin.

Wang Zong-yue is credited with writing the *Yin Fu Spear Chronicle*, and according to the preface he lived in Luo Yang in 1791, and in 1795 was in Kaifeng working as a teacher and scholar. These are both in Henan province and near the Chen village. The Chens place him as a contemporary of their thirteenth generation member, Chen Bing-wang, who taught the *Pao Chui* method to Chen Chang-xing. If these dates are accurate, it would make it possible for Wang to have taught Tai Chi Chuan to Chen Chang-xing, or for Wang to have taught Jiang Fa who in turn taught Chen Chang-xing. This contradicts Chen historians such as Tang Hao who have suggested that Wang learned his art from the Chen clan; there is no evidence for this claim.

Wu Tu-nan records how he made a number of trips to Bao Ji, which is a bit more than three hours by train to the west of Xian. There, in the Taoist Temple of the Golden Pavilion, can be found a number of items and rooms identifying Chang San-feng with the temple. Wu records that the priests in the temple still practised a form of Tai Chi Chuan handed down from Chang San-feng which they taught to a man from Xian named Wang Zong, and styled Wang Zong-yue. Xian is seventeen hours west of the Chen village by train. As no temple records were available for Wu to inspect, we only have his word to go on. I visited the temple in 1995 and there is certainly a strong Chang San-feng connection. However, there is a problem with the name Wang Zong.

Wang Zong (yue) and *Nei Jia Chuan*

The sinologist, Arthur Waley, identified the first use of the term *Nei Dan* or Internal Alchemy – referring to Chinese techniques designed to promote health and tranquillity – as occurring in a Chan Buddhist text of c565 AD where *Nei Dan* was said to be stimulated by *Wai Dan* (External Alchemy). Chan Buddhism was heavily influenced by Taoist ideas and terminology, so it is not surprising that *Nei Jia* has long been used to refer to Taoist-influenced hygienic exercise and martial arts; given references in the work of Lao Tzu, Chuang Tzu and others, such arts existed prior to 300 BC.

Tai Chi Chuan is one of the three major schools jointly referred to as Internal Boxing (*Nei Jia Chuan*) (the others are *Ba Gua* and *Xing Yi*); Yang Lu-chan was the first person we know of to use the term Tai Chi Chuan when he came to Beijing around 1852. The old names given for it include Long Boxing (*Chang Chuan*), Cotton Boxing (*Mian Chuan*), Neutralizing Boxing (*Hua Chuan*), the Thirteen Tactics (*Shi San Shi*) and Internal Family Boxing (*Nei Jia Chuan*). However, references to any and all of these terms are not necessarily references to Tai Chi Chuan.

There are special reasons for the use of the term *Nei Jia Chuan* in connection with Tai Chi Chuan. First there is the idea of hidden aspects of the art which one is taught only after ritual initiation. Second, there is the emphasis on the mind/intent, the spiritual, on strengthening the body internally, and on attacking the opponent's energy system by sealing, grasping, twisting or striking vital points. Third, there is the use of a special vocabulary borrowed in parts from Taoist ideas about circulation in *Nei Dan*. Fourth, Taoism is Chinese as opposed to Buddhism, introduced to China from India.

Xie Ting-fei's *Chen Shi Taiji Pao Chui Quan* published in Taipei in 1985 refers to Huang Zong-xi, also styled Li-zhou, as being a student of Wang Zheng-nan. In the eighth year of the reign of the Emperor Kang Xi (1669), Huang wrote on Wang's tombstone:

> Shaolin boxing is famous in the world and concentrates on attacking the opponent's weak points. People can therefore take advantage of this. In the so-called 'Nei Jia' (Internal Family), stillness is used to control movement; when the opponent attacks, then he is countered. So Shaolin is called Wai Jia (External Family). The origins (of Nei Jia) are mainly from Chang San-feng. San-feng was a Wudang Taoist. The Emperor Hui Zong (1101–25 AD) sent for him, but though he arrived, he did not succeed in meeting the Emperor. In a dream Chang was taught boxing by the Emperor Yuan Di and the next day he killed more than a hundred bandits by himself.

Despite the absurdity of the last sentence, the inscription is notable because it shows that the concept of *Nei Jia Chuan* already existed at the time of the *Chuan Ching*, and that even then Chang San-feng was believed to be the founder. Mention of the Emperor Hui Zong sending for Chang is strange, because his heyday seems to have been from the mid-fourteenth to the early fifteenth century (although it is possible that there was more than one Chang San-feng and/or that one or more of these records is wrong).

The inscription says that the art became popular in Shaanxi one hundred years after Chang San-feng, with Wang Zong being the most outstanding exponent. He taught Chen Zhou-tong from Wen Zhou. During the Jia Jing period (1522–66) of the Ming dynasty, Chang Song-xi from Hai Yan was the most famous exponent. Chang taught Ye Ji-mei and Jin Quan. The latter taught Shan Si-nan who transmitted the art to Wang Zheng-nan from Ching Shan Zhi and others.

A criticism often laid against these references to Chang San-feng is that Tai Chi Chuan is not mentioned. However, this may be because the term was not used for the art until much later. Tai Chi Chuan today is still referred to as *Nei Jia Chuan* and 'shadow boxing'.

In the *Ning Po Prefecture Gazetteer*, the claim is made that Chang Song-xi practised *Nei Jia Chuan* and that he was a disciple of Chang San-feng who is referred to as an alchemist from Wudang Mountain. This is quite impossible, as we'll see later, because the dates are incompatible.

The Northern and Southern Schools of Tai Chi Chuan

Many Tai Chi historians used the inscription and the similarity in the names of Wang Zong and Wang Zong-yue to claim that Wang Zong's *Nei Jia Chuan* was in fact Tai Chi Chuan and that there was a northern school of Tai Chi Chuan which was passed from Wang Zong (-yue) to Jiang Fa and thus to Chen Chang-xing, while Chang Song-xi and his line were the southern school of Tai Chi Chuan.

Wang Zong was from Guan Zhong in Shaanxi province where the major city is Xian, while the later Wang Zong-yue was from Shan You in Shanxi province. These two provinces have similar sounding names, although the characters are different; also Shaanxi is to the west of Henan where the Chen village is situated, while Shanxi is to the north of Henan province. So it seems that either the two have been confused, or someone has deliberately linked them. At best we can say that there was a northern and a southern school of *Nei Jia Chuan* which may have been linked, because the basic theory is similar.

It was thought until recently that only the northern school through Jiang Fa still survived, but Wang Wei-shen's *Wudang Chang Song-xi Pai Nei Jia Chuan* (Wudang Chang Song-xi School Internal Family Boxing) claims that the southern school survived and was transmitted to Wang who became the twentieth generation versed in the art. Wang was born in 1913 and learned through two masters, the latter of whom, Li Hao-tian, was a Wudang Mountain Taoist.

Wang claims the Ming dynasty Chang San-feng as the founder, maintaining that Chang taught Wang Zong from Shaanxi province and that Wang taught Chen Zhou-tong. Chen passed the art down through Chang Song-xi, who used the essence of eight different martial arts to create the Wudang Chang Song-xi School of Internal Boxing. For this to tally with the grave inscription there would have to be other instructors between Chang San-feng and Wang Zong, between Wang Zong

and Chang Song-xi, and between Chang Song-xi and later generations in the lineage.

While there is an internal element to the training, there is much in the book that is different in theory and practice from Tai Chi Chuan, perhaps reflecting the essence of the other styles which Chang Song-xi combined with *Nei Jia Chuan*. There are no references to the Tai Chi Chuan classics.

A number of writers have suggested that Shan Si-nan and Huang Zong-xi were expert in *Dim Mak* – the art of attacking vital points – and this is certainly part of the Tai Chi Chuan syllabus. Furthermore, as Professor Douglas Wile has shown in *Lost T'ai-chi Classics of The Ch'ing Dynasty*, a number of key phrases used by *Nei Jia Chuan* stylists such as Chang Nai-zhou are found in the Tai Chi Chuan classics.

Japanese Ju Jutsu – literally soft technique/art – traced its origins from a Chinese named Chen Yuan-pin (1587–1674). The similarity of the theory and techniques handed down by Chen to those of Tai Chi Chuan/*Nei Jia Chuan*, and the fact that he was a contemporary of Wang Zheng-nan, all suggest that *Nei Jia Chuan* once exercised a profound influence on martial arts in China and Japan, in the same way that Tai Chi Chuan does today.

The Third Outsider: Jiang Fa

Many Yang lineage histories say that Chen Chang-xing (1771–1853) was taught by Jiang Fa, who in turn was taught by Wang Zong-yue, and that this was the northern school lineage of Tai Chi Chuan. Wang Zong-yue is also supposed to have handed down the southern school of Tai

Chi Chuan through Chang Song-xi. However, even if we accept the Chen story that Jiang Fa was a contemporary of the tenth generation of the Chen family, this would make him a young man in the year 1650, about twenty years before the death of Wang Zheng-nan. Yet the latter was the great grandstudent of Wang Zong who was supposed to be Jiang's master. Almost certainly Wang Zong and Wang Zong-yue have been made into one person, when in fact they were from different provinces and different eras.

Chen historians Chen Xin and Gu Liu-xin acknowledge the existence of Jiang Fa, but have him learning from Chen Wang-ting who was teaching his system of boxing around 1650. Yang lineage systems list Jiang Fa as the teacher of Chen Chang-xing (1771–1853) – a disparity in dates of about 150 years.

The Chens have Wang Zong-yue as a contemporary of the Chen clan's thirteenth generation. If so, he could have taught Jiang Fa and even Chen Chang-xing, provided the Yangs are right about Jiang's dates. The Chen material does not say who, if anyone, learned from Wang and Jiang, as according to them all lines of transmission of the Chen art are through Chen clansmen until the time of Yang Lu-chan.

All Yang family lineages, except that of Wu Yu-xiang, list Wang Zong-yue as the teacher of Jiang Fa, and Jiang as the teacher of Chen Chang-xing. Even the Wus acknowledge Wang's involvement. What motive could there be for fabricating what was then recent and hence verifiable history? Furthermore, there is evidence from Tang Hao that Chen Xin in the 1930s was trying to suppress rumours amongst Chen villagers that Jiang Fa taught Chen Chang-xing.

Wu Tu-nan says that he was told by Chen Xin that every year, after the harvest, clan members would gather in the village yard to practise Shaolin boxing. Chen Xin said that one autumn Chen Chang-xing was leading his sons, nephews and disciples through their training in the yard when a watching stranger gave out a laugh. The stranger turned to leave, but Chen Chang-xing ran after him and grabbed him by the shoulder, only to be thrown to the ground. Chen got up and begged to be accepted as a pupil.

The stranger was Jiang Fa, who ran a beancurd business in Xian and who was passing through on his way to visit his mother in Henan province. They arranged to meet again in three years time, and then Chen Chang-xing went through *Bai Shi* (ritual initiation) with Jiang, prior to learning Tai Chi Chuan.This may have been in the 1800s. Wu met another villager, Du Yu-wen, who confirmed that Chen Tai Chi had come from Jiang Fa from Kaifeng in Henan province (remember that in 1795 Wang Zong-yue was supposed to have been in Kaifeng). Wu states that the names of the styles and the sequence practised by Du were the same as those taught by Yang Lu-chan.

There still exist a few poems attributed to Jiang Fa which give advice on Tai Chi Chuan training in verse, but the ones I have seen are not as detailed or as impressive as the Tai Chi Chuan classics, and seem derivative.

If Jiang did learn Tai Chi Chuan from Wang Zong-yue, the Chens' dates for Jiang are wrong. This suggests Jiang learned Tai Chi Chuan before 1795 when Wang published the *Yin Fu Spear Treatise*, and then Jiang passed on the art to Chen Chang-xing. This solution agrees with the dates we have for Wang Zong-yue and Chen Chang-xing, and backs up the historical tradition of the Yang Lu-chan lineage.

The Zhao Bao Village

The Zhao Bao style consists of so-called new small-frame two *Tao Lu*, said by the Chens to have been developed by Chen You-ben in the Chen village and passed on to his relative Chen Qing-ping (1795–1868) who married into the nearby Zhao Bao village. Qing-ping was a contemporary of Yang Lu-chan and must have known him.

Wu Yu-xiang (1812–80) is the only student of Yang Lu-chan we know of to visit the Zhao Bao village. Wu's nephew, Li Yi-yu, claims Wu spent about a month there learning all Qing-ping's secrets.

The practitioners I talked to when I visited the village in 1995 said that they did not *Bai Shi*. The Zhao Baos have their own identity and trace their line of transmission from Jiang Fa (though they are inconsistent on his dates), while the Chen family has Chen Qing-ping learning from Chen You-ben. The logical explanation is that what Chen Qing-ping learned from You-ben was *Pao Chui* and that he learned Tai Chi Chuan later from Chen Chang-xing or Jiang Fa. I suspect also that not only did Qing-ping teach Wu, but that there was an exchange, and so the Zhao Bao style is a halfway house between Chen and Yang, nearer the former in terms of the syllabus, and nearer the latter in terms of the way in which the form is done.

The Zhao Bao form in execution is more similar to that of the Yang lineage, being softer and smoother than the Chen method though the techniques resemble the Chen style more. The martial aspect of their art seems to rely largely on applying moving pushing hands principles.

Conclusions on Tai Chi Chuan and the Chen village

We have seen not only inconsistencies, but a large-scale rewriting of history by the Chens, mixing one Chen Wang-ting with another and removing all the old gravestones. The evidence for Chen Wang-ting as the founder of Tai Chi Chuan is almost entirely based on the writings of Chen Xin, the earliest verifiable writer on Chen style, and his collaborators. Yet Wu Tu-nan alleges that in 1917 not only did Chen Xin admit that he did not know any Tai Chi Chuan, but also that the art came to the village from Jiang Fa. Even among the Chen clan his reputation is as a writer about, rather than as a practitioner of their art. In content, theory and method of practice, the Chen system differs vastly from the Yang lineage.

Fig 20 Chen villager in the family training hall demonstrates Sparrow Ground Dragon.

45

Authorship of all five major Tai Chi classics is traditionally ascribed to either Chang San-feng or Wang Zong-yue; the Chen clan does not claim authorship of any of them. The dates for Wang in Kaifeng and Luoyang match those for Chen Chang-xing, and therefore also match the Chen clan dates for him and the Yang lineage dates for the shadowy figure of Jiang Fa.

The Chens' training area is in the open at the end of the village street. The house where Chen Chang-xing taught Tai Chi Chuan is at the other end of the street behind high walls. Chen Chang-xing is not honoured in the Chen training hall; he has no gravestone. He is only commemorated in the house of Chen De-hu. Wu Tu-nan was told that Chen Chang-xing was considered a disgrace to the Chen clan because he went through *Bai Shi* with an outsider, Jiang Fa, and was forbidden to continue teaching *Pao Chui*. All this points to two styles being taught in the one village: *Pao Chui* in the yard and Tai Chi Chuan behind closed doors.

Finally, members of the Chen clan served with the Red Army and their village was used as a base by the Red Army during the Revolution. The Communist Party orthodoxy could not accept that Tai Chi Chuan was founded by Chang San-feng, so until the downfall of the Gang of Four, they supported the Chen line that Chen Wang-ting was the founder and linked him to the more famous general with a similar name.

The evidence suggests that Tai Chi Chuan was passed on from Wang Zong-yue in Kaifeng to Jiang Fa, and from the latter to Chen Chang-xing. Wang and Jiang may have taught other Chen clansmen, but there are no records of this in any of the lineage histories.

TAI CHI CHUAN BEFORE WANG ZONG-YUE

Let us now look at Tai Chi Chuan before the time of Wang Zong-yue. As we have seen, in 1669 Wang Zheng-nan's student, Huang Zong-xi, wrote on his master's tombstone:

> In the so-called '*Nei Jia*' stillness is used to control movement; when the opponent attacks then he is countered. Therefore Shaolin is called *Wai Jia* (External Family).

We have a similar reference in the biography of Chang Song-xi.

Like Tai Chi Chuan, *Nei Jia Chuan* is contrasted with Shaolin; like Tai Chi Chuan it is a counter-attacking method, it also uses the terminology of employing stillness to defeat movement, and it traces the origins of the art from Chang San-feng – though not perhaps the same Chang San-feng.

Professor Douglas Wile in his *Lost T'ai-chi Classics* lists a scholar and martial artist, Chang Nai-chou (c1742), in Si-Shui in Henan province who practised *Nei Jia Chuan* and whose writings contain a number of phrases also found in the Tai Chi Chuan classics. This provides a link with Huang Zong-xi's inscription in 1669, and Wang Zong-yue who was in Henan province in 1791–5. Although we cannot prove that these three strands were one art, we now have definite evidence of a continuing *Nei Jia Chuan* tradition from the early seventeenth century to the present day.

CHANG SAN-FENG

Who was Chang San-feng? When did he live? What is his connection with Tai Chi Chuan? Who was his teacher?

Wong Shiu-hon in his paper *On the Cult of Chang San-feng* deduced that Chang lived in the Ming dynasty between the Yen Yu period (1314–20) and the seventeenth year of Yung Lo (1419). Wong and others have researched the date of 1247 AD given for Chang's birth by some historians, and have suggested that this earlier date is probably a result of confusion over the identity of Chang's father. From the fifteenth century onwards Chang was rather conveniently identified with a whole range of Taoists and eccentrics, some of whom date back as early as the twelfth century.

Chang is described as having an unusual and dishevelled appearance, earning

Fig 21   Chang San-feng, the filthy Taoist.

him the nickname of '*La Ta*', or 'filthy'. He had long ear lobes and large eyes as befits a sage, and was very tall. He came from what is now Liao Yang in Liao Ning province in the far north-east of China.

In 1431 Chang is mentioned by Ren Zi-yuan in his *Tai Yue Tai He Shan Zhi* (*Annals of Supreme Summit Supreme Harmony* (ie Wudang) *Mountain*) as giving instructions to five disciples on Wudang Mountain during the Hung Wu period (1368–98). This is the earliest literary reference I have come across for Chang. However, none of the five names listed by Ren correspond with any of the names mentioned in the Tai Chi Chuan or *Nei Jia* lineages – although this is not necessarily significant, as a master could have hundreds or even thousands of disciples in a lifetime.

Wang Xi-ling (1664–1724) wrote a number of works on Chang San-feng, one of which is entitled *San Feng Zu Shi Quan Ji Xu* (*Complete Record of Founder San Feng*). The term '*Zu Shi*' means 'founder', and is the way that Chang is referred to in a mantra taught to Tai Chi Chuan students after *Bai Shi* (ritual initiation). Wang belonged to a Taoist '*Men*' or sect of Chang San-feng, and students who have gone through *Bai Shi* are referred to as '*Men Ren*'. Wang claimed to have met and received instruction from Chang, but this is not possible given their respective dates; it is more likely that Wang summoned Chang's spirit through '*Fu Qi*' or planchette writing.

The scholar and mystic Wang Shi-zhen (1634–1711) refers, in the *Complete Records of Chang San-feng* to Chang as being a practitioner of *Nei Jia Chuan*, corroborating the inscription of Huang Zong-xi written on Wang Zheng-nan's gravestone. The *Complete Records* contains poetry attributed to Chang referring to Yin and Yang in the field of sexual physiological alchemy and linked to the concept of 'the tree without root' (*Wu Gen Shu*). Chang has a reputation as an alchemist, but what kind of Taoist was he? Did he take part in exorcisms, planchette writing, casting spells, was he involved in Taoist sexual practices and martial arts?

The *Chang San-feng Lie Chuan* (*Biography of Chang San-feng*) attributed to Lu Xi-xing (died 1601) has Chang learning from a Master Huo Long (Fire Dragon), who was in turn the student of the famous Chen Duan who is credited with inventing the Tai Chi Diagram on which Zhou Dun-yi based his *Tai Chi Tu Shuo* (*Diagrammatic Explanation of the Tai Chi Diagram*). However, the dates do not correspond, although it is possible that Huo Long was part of a tradition involving Chen Duan; it could be that he was a member of the Tai Chi Diagram sect, and that he passed on his knowledge to Chang San-feng.

CHANG SAN-FENG: THE IMPERIAL CONNECTION

In 1372 Emperor Tai Zu sent for Chang. In 1407 Emperor Cheng Zu dispatched an expedition under High Commissioner Hu Yong which spent nine years searching for Chang. He sent another expedition to search for the elusive sage from 1419–23, as well as four further messengers. Cheng Zu also built the 'Palace for Encountering the Immortal Chang' in Chang's honour.

Fig 22   Imperial tablet dedicated to Chang San-feng at the Temple of the Golden Pavilion.

The carving on a stone tablet in the Golden Pavilion Temple in Bao Ji, erected at imperial expense in Chang's memory, states that it was begun in 1434 and finished in 1446. In 1459 the Ying Zong emperor issued an imperial decree honouring Chang San-feng.

Looking again at the inscription written by Huang Zong-xi in 1669:

> ...The origins (of *Nei Jia*) are mainly from Chang San-feng. San-feng was a Wudang Taoist. The Emperor Hui Zong (1101–25 AD) sent for him, but though he arrived, he did not succeed in meeting the Emperor.

Either there were two Chang San-fengs, or Huang has made a mistake, as the overwhelming evidence for the existence of the famous Chang San-feng points to him as being active in the late fourteenth and early fifteenth centuries, not the twelfth.

The character for '*San*' in his given name means 'three'. In most books the character for '*feng*' in Chang's name is that meaning 'abundance', and sometimes it is given in its full form, sometimes in its simplified form. So we have 'Chang of The Three Abundances'. 'Feng' is the name of the fifty-fifth hexagram of the *Book of Changes*. The full form of the '*feng*' character had the original meaning of a 'ritual vessel used for offerings of grain'. The simplified form for '*feng*' is used in the imperial inscription referring to Chang San-feng at the Golden Pavilion Temple in Bao Ji, while the character used for '*feng*' in Huang's inscription on Wang Zheng-nan's gravestone is different, and means the 'peak of a hill'. There are suggestions that the latter was chosen by Chang as a pen name in reference to three peaks around the Golden Pavilion Temple. Others suggest

that this was a reference to three of Wudang Mountain's seventy-two peaks.

There are other possibilities. First, the Golden Pavilion Temple in Bao Ji has three '*feng*' or ritual sacrificial vessels for offerings to the gods. Second, the name '*San Feng*' or 'Three Abundances' could, if we accept that Chang was a Taoist alchemist, be a reference to the Three Treasures of *Qi*, *Jing* and *Shen*.

In his *Tai Chi Chuan Hui Pian* (*Collection of Writings on Tai Chi Chuan*) Cheng Wing-kwong lists Chang San-feng as the founder of *Xian Jia Baduanjin* (*Immortal Family Eight Pieces of Brocade*) as well as Tai Chi Chuan. *Baduanjin* and other Taoist hygienic exercises have been practised for more than 2,000 years. One of the exercises is specifically sexual in nature, and this matches suggestions in a number of works from the sixteenth century onwards that Chang San-feng was an expert in physiological alchemy.

Qiang Shao-shu, writing in the seventeenth century, says Chang San-feng was involved with the painter Huang Gong-wang in the 1330s, with the Quan Zhen (Complete Truth) Taoist sect. The titles of at least two of the sect's treatises include the expression *Bao Yi*, or 'Embracing the One'. This is the name of one of the twenty-four Tai Chi *Nei Kung* exercises as well as a quotation from Lao Tzu's *Tao Te Ching*, '...The sage embraces the One...' The meaning of *Bao Yi* in this context is 'to embrace unity with the *Tao*'.

Anna Seidel in an essay on Chang San-feng in *Self and Society in Ming Thought* refers to a thirteenth-century treatise on physiological alchemy which mentions and warns against a method of sexual intercourse known as *San Feng Huang Gu Zhi Shu* (Art of The Three Peaks and Yellow Valley). Did Chang San-feng take his name from this, or is it just coincidence? Or could this be a reference to an earlier Chang San-feng, perhaps the one mentioned on Wang Zheng-nan's gravestone?

Wudang Mountain is the home of the True Warrior – the legendary Emperor Zhen Wu. The name 'Wudang' means 'Match the Warrior', and the Wudang priests have a long reputation for martial ability: in 1984 I witnessed a demonstration of *Tai He Chuan* (Supreme Harmony Boxing) by an octogenarian priest. A form of Tai Chi Chuan is practised on the mountain which bears little resemblance to Yang lineage systems, although a number of postures in Wudang *Qi Gong* have the same names as Tai Chi Chuan techniques, for example White Crane Flaps Its Wings, The Peng Spreading Its Wings. According to Wu Tu-nan, who visited both places, in a tradition dating from the time Chang San-feng lived at them, Tai Chi was also practised at the Temple of the Golden Pavilion at Bao Ji and the White Cloud Temple in Beijing.

Conclusion

As we have said, it is possible that there was more than one Chang San-feng. I believe on the available evidence that there was one Chang San-feng who in the mid-fourteenth century became famous as a Taoist. Earlier dates are likely to be due to carelessness, or to confusing him with others, or to give him greater antiquity as befits a sage.

Academics have suggested that Chang San-feng was selected as the founder of Tai Chi Chuan and other Taoist arts because of his connection with Zhen Wu on Wudang Mountain, and also to give these arts the same kudos that Shaolin Boxing possessed by having the Indian monk Bodhidharma (fifth century AD) as the founder. However, Taoist martial arts and Taoist health practices existed for centuries before Chang, so why was a relatively obscure and more recent figure such as Chang selected as founder? Why not go back a thousand years before Bodhidharma to Lao Tzu or Chuang Tzu, both of whom wrote on many of the concepts which we use in Tai Chi Chuan today?

Wudang Mountain has been connected with Taoists from at least the second century BC, and Wudang Taoists have long been the most martial. Written

Fig 23   Altar dedicated to Chang San-feng in the Golden Pavilion Temple, Bao Ji.

sources and relics on the mountain suggest that Chang San-feng was part of this tradition. Also, when I went to the Golden Pavilion Temple at Bao Ji in 1995, Mr Ma Jian, a superb artist who has been the caretaker since the 1950s, told me that there had been a martial tradition at the temple up to the time of the Cultural Revolution with monks practising Tai Chi Chuan handed down by Chang San-feng.

This raises a strong possibility that Yang lineage systems are correct in claiming that Chang was involved in the creation of the art we now call Tai Chi Chuan. This art has all the elements of Taoistic practice, including physiological alchemy, ritual initiation, oral formulas and tradition, Taoistic terminology, and a theoretical and symbolical element drawn largely, though not exclusively, from Taoist philosophy and religion. All these elements exist in Tai Chi Chuan and existed ·in the heyday of Chang San-feng. Finally, the oral tradition from teacher to teacher is that Chang was the founder, and this is why the *Bai Shi* ceremony is done in front of his portrait.

TAOIST MARTIAL ARTS BEFORE CHANG SAN FENG

Wu Tu-nan tells of acquiring *Song Style Family Tai Chi Kung Source and History Clan Analects* around 1908–9. The book was written on yellowed and brittle paper. Wu copied it for others including his masters, Wu Jian-chuan and Yang Shao-hou, and for the Tai Chi historian Xu Yu-sheng.

Shortly after this, Song Shu-ming, secretary to General Yuan Shi-Kai, came to Beijing claiming to be a descendant of Song Yuan-qiao. He produced a copy of the same book which Wu Tu-nan had been given, except that Song's copy was entitled *Song Yuan-qiao Tai Chi Kung Source and History Clan Analects*; Song claimed that his ancestor Yuan-qiao had written it after learning Tai Chi Chuan from Chang San-feng.

In Song Yuan-qiao's book, he or whoever wrote it claims that he went with six others including our old friend, Chang Song-xi, of the southern school of *Nei Jia Chuan*, to meet a Master (Fu Zi) Li on Wudang Mountain. They failed to find Li, but met Chang San-feng at the Temple of the Jade Void. Chang was the master of Chang Song-xi and Chang Cui-shan, and from that time on, the seven visited Wudang annually to train in Tai Chi Chuan with Chang San-feng.

The Master Li they were (rather optimistically) searching for was Li Tao-zi of the Tang dynasty (618–958) who passed on Before Heaven Boxing (*Xian Tian Chuan*) to the Yu clan including Yu Ching-wei (two Yus were among the intrepid seven). A note was appended to the book stating that a Master Li, whom they later encountered, was a person of the late Yuan and early Ming (c. thirteenth century) and not Li Tao-zi. Li Tao-zi was known as Li Tao-shan (Li of the Mountain of The Way) perhaps because he lived in the Southern Cliff Palace on Wudang Mountain.

The book said that as early as the Liang dynasty (502–557 AD), Prefect Cheng Ling-xi from Xi Zhou in Anhui province practised Tai Chi Chuan. The art was taught to troops and for several generations within Cheng's family, to his descendant Cheng Mi, a scholar and expert on the *Book of Changes*. Cheng Mi claimed that his ancestor Ling-xi was taught Tai Chi Chuan by Han Gong-yue and that the art had existed long before this. Ling-xi added elbow techniques and named the art Little Nine Heavens (*Xiao Jiu Tian*), referring to the eight directions and the centre that is, the Eight Trigrams with the Tai Chi symbol in the centre. A martial method with this name and Taoist origins is still practised in north-east China.

The book went on to say that a giant, hirsute, Taoist recluse named Xu Xuan-ping, a contemporary of the great Tang poet Li Bai (701–762 AD), resided in Xi Zhou, Zi Yang Mountain in Anhui province, and taught a Tai Chi Chuan method called Thirty-Seven Styles (*San Shi Qi Sh* – some give the name as Three Generations Seven which sounds the same in Chinese), also known as Long Boxing. Xu composed the following poem:

> Carrying firewood on my back at dawn I go to sell it.
> Buying wine I return at dusk
> I ask where is my home?
> Pierce the clouds and enter the verdant hills.

Xu is mentioned in a text called *Chang San-feng Cheng Liu* (*The Chang San-feng Inheritance*), part of a body of writings which Wu Jian-chuan's sons claim were given to their family by Yang Ban-hou. The text purports to have been written by Chang and mentions Xu as having passed the art down. If Ban-hou gave the Wus this text it must have been before 1892, and it therefore predates and corroborates Song's book. However, such texts are notorious for their lack of reliability.

Finally we have After Heaven Boxing taught by Yin Li-xiang to Hu Jing-zi and Song Zhong-shu. Little is known of Yin, but there is a poem attributed to him written en route to the city of Yangzhou:

> Lastingly as Heaven and Earth, let us be at our leisure
> Since you are without care, let me also be at rest
> Roaming to where the waves break and to the limits of Heaven, none bother us
> Spring winds come, I play the flute upstairs in the tavern.

These arts show a connection in terminology, which is Taoist; in time, since at least three of the arts were being practised during the Tang dynasty; and in geographical location, namely Wudang Mountain and Anhui. This fits in with what we know from poetry and other writings of the interchange of ideas and techniques between hermits, poets, knight errants and others in Taoist dwellings, in taverns and on the road.

However, we can't be sure that these arts existed, though a number of the personages listed as being involved in their transmission are historical figures. As is the case with Chang San-feng, there is no definite proof of their involvement with martial arts in general and with Tai Chi Chuan in particular, but why select relatively obscure provincials to be Tai Chi patriarchs?

The book repeats the story mentioned earlier in the *Biography of Chang San-feng* attributed to Lu Xi-xing, that Chang learned Tai Chi Chuan on Mount Hua from our old friend Huo Long (whose real name, Wu Tu-nan says, was Jia De-sheng). Huo Long was taught by Chen Xi-yi, a philosopher contemporary of Chu Xi (1130–1200 AD) and a descendant of Chen Duan, both famous philosophers.

Chen Duan is credited with developing the Tai Chi Diagram and the Before Heaven Diagram; he also lived on Wudang Mountain as well as Mount Hua. Furthermore Chang San-feng was supposedly already in his sixties when learning from Huo Long. Let us look at this information in the light of what we have deduced about Chang San-feng: we can see the dates do not correspond, although it is possible that Huo Long was part of a tradition involving Chen Duan – perhaps being a member of the Tai Chi Diagram sect – and that he passed on his knowledge to Chang San-feng.

First, if Huo Long had learned from a contemporary of Chu Xi, then this would at the latest have been at the end of the twelfth century. And if, as the book states, he then taught Chang San-feng, this would have to have been, at the latest, in the mid-thirteenth century – yet we have seen that Chang San-feng was active in the mid-fourteenth and early fifteenth century.

Second, the book has Chang Song-xi and others visiting Chang San-feng. This is at variance with what Wang Wei-shen has to say in *Wudang Chang Song-xi Pai Nei Jia Chuan*. Wang has Chang Song-xi living from about 1506 until 1620 and learning the art from Chen Zhou-tong, who in turn learned from Wang Zong. This tallies with the fact that Chang Song-xi's grand-student Wang Zheng-nan died (as we have seen) in 1669. Yet Song's book has Chang Song-xi going to Wudang Mountain and learning from Chang San-feng about two hundred years before this.

Song Shu-ming's book is of doubtful historical accuracy, yet it gives us possible clues about how Tai Chi Chuan may have developed in and from a Taoist philosophical context, why the name Tai Chi Chuan was adopted, and the quotations from the philosophers Chen Duan and Zhou Dun-yi in the Tai Chi Chuan Canon (*Ching*). Zhou is noteworthy as he was also an authority on Taoist physiological alchemy.

Taoism has a history of well over 2,000 years, and Chinese physiological alchemy can be dated back to well before the present era. Chinese martial arts have an even longer history, so for these elements to have come together by the time of the Liang or Tang dynasty would hardly be surprising.

TAI CHI CHUAN: BEIJING AND BEYOND

Having dealt with Tai Chi Chuan history at and before the time of Yang Lu-chan, let us address Tai Chi Chuan's development from the time of Yang Lu-chan up to the present day. Let us first look at what influences he came across when he arrived in Beijing.

Ba Gua, Xing Yi and Tai Chi Chuan

Ba Gua and *Xing Yi* are the other two arts which, with Tai Chi Chuan, are commonly referred to as *Nei Jia Chuan* and sometimes as *Wudang* in reference to the mountain of that name and in contrast to *Shaolin*. There are as many stories and mysteries surrounding the origins and development of these arts, as there are in the case of Tai Chi Chuan. Let us look at some of the parallels between the arts.

First there is a common thread in location. As we have seen, the Chen village is in Henan province while Yang Lu-chan came from Hebei. Dong Hai-chuan who brought what he called *Ba Gua Zhang* (Eight Trigram Palm) to Beijing around 1856 also came from Hebei province and also served the Manchu royal family, as did a number of his disciples. A contemporary of Dong in Beijing was Guo Yun-shen, a master of the Hebei school of *Xing Yi Chuan* (Form and Intent Boxing).

So here we have masters of each of the major *Nei Jia Chuan* arts, all in Beijing at the same time, and all from the Hebei province, with at least two of them connected to the Manchu royal family. Coincidence?

We will look at the theory and nomenclature of *Ba Gua Zhang* and *Xing Yi* in comparison with that of Tai Chi Chuan in a later chapter. Suffice it to say that there are numerous similarities. In application, *Ba Gua Zhang* tends to be circular with quick steps and changing palms, whereas *Xing Yi* tends to be direct, using the fist. Tai Chi Chuan uses both these approaches.

What we can deduce from all this is that the *Nei Jia Chuan* tradition was particularly strong in the 1850s in Henan and Hebei provinces, and that the different *Nei Jia Chuan* traditions must have influenced one another at least when they met in Beijing, if not considerably earlier. We can only speculate on how much Yang Lu-chan and his successors changed their Tai Chi Chuan in response to this and other influences. It is said that a teacher's worth can be gauged from the ability of his students, so let us look at Yang's lineage.

THE YANG LU-CHAN LINEAGE

The Sons

Yang had three sons and at least one daughter. I can find no records of Yang's eldest son accompanying him to Beijing or being involved with Tai Chi Chuan, and I have come across no information on the daughter having practised or taught the art, so we are left with the other two sons, Yang Ban-hou (1837–92) and Yang Jian-hou (1839–1917) who would have been teenagers when their father came to teach in Beijing.

Yang Ban-hou was known by his father's nickname of 'Invincible Yang'. Yet the well known American Tai Chi teacher, T.T. Liang, relates in *Tai Chi Chuan for Health and Self Defence* that one of Yang Lu-chan's senior students, Chen Xiu-feng, publicly humiliated both Yang's sons at Yang's burial in 1872 by taking the title of head disciple of the second generation of Yang Tai Chi, and offering publicly in front of the brothers to accept challenges from anyone who disputed his right to this title. Neither son dared to dispute with him because Chen's skill was so superior to theirs, yet this would be a time when both brothers should have been in their prime

There are many other stories of how their father forced them to train, of the harshness of Ban-hou's teaching and how he could not keep students. Apart from the members of the Manchu royal family who were able to go through *Bai Shi* directly with Yang Lu-chan, it is said that all other students had to *Bai Shi* with Ban-hou as they could not be allowed to be on the same footing as royalty. His main student seems to have been his nephew Yang Shao-hou who had a similar reputation to his uncle.

Some people claim to be practising the old Yang Lu-chan form, but since he died well over a century ago and there are no photographs or videos of him practising, we have no way of knowing what that was. Some say he modified the form to remove jumps, stamping and explosive action, others say that his descendants or students of the other Yang lineage members did so also; but in a number of Tai Chi systems from the Yang Lu-chan lineage, these types of movement exist in the weapon forms.

Most so-called Yang-style Tai Chi Chuan now being practised comes from Yang Jian-hou's lineage, and in particular from his youngest son, Yang Cheng-fu (1883–1936). We know from the writings of Cheng-fu's students that he changed his style at least three times during his teaching career – although this is hardly surprising since in his later years he was enormously fat; he died at the age of fifty-three.

The Yang family are supposed to have evolved three methods of practising the form: Yang Ban-hou did small frame which was lively with higher stances; Yang Jian-hou, who sems to have been a milder character, practiced medium frame; and his son Yang Cheng-fu taught large frame with longer stances and more expansive movements. There are some writings at least partly attributed to Ban-hou, and I will deal with these separately.

Yang-Style Tai Chi Chuan Today

In an interview on his first visit to the United States, Zhen-duo, third son of Yang Cheng-fu, was asked if the Yang family style had a fast form or a two person form; he said that there were no such forms in the Yang system. In fact these forms are respectively practised in the styles of Cheng-fu's students, Tung Ying-jie and Cheng Man-ching, so either they are no longer taught by the Yang family, or Cheng-fu's students got them from elsewhere. Tung claimed to have learned his fast form, besides other

methods which make Tung style distinctive, from Li Xiang-yuan, a student of Hao Wei-zhen.

How effective is the Yang family system today as a fighting art? Since the time of Ban-hou there have been no famous fighters in the Yang family; this is not to say they have no fighting ability, but in comparison with the abilities of their ancestors and others. Cheng-fu is widely known to have been bested in his later years by the late great Wan Lai-sheng of Natural Boxing (*Zi Ren Chuan*). Why should this be?

With the overthrow of the old dynasty and the establishment of the Republic, members of the third generation of the Yang family found that the best source of revenue was to teach wealthy members of the *literati* and merchant classes who wanted the health and aesthetic aspects of the art rather than the martial ones. Also, rather than having to prove themselves and their art, later generations of the family rested on the laurels of the first two generations.

In books and film showing Yang Cheng-fu and his students applying self-defence techniques, four things are noticeable. First, the techniques are done almost exactly as they appear in the form. Second, there is little or no evasion involved in the applications. Third, there are few throwing techniques. Fourth, most of the techniques are far from practical. Why?

I believe that probably some applications were hidden, but also that much was forgotten and so techniques were reinvented to fit the moves in the form. Because of his bulk, many of the evasion skills and more gymnastically demanding techniques were no longer an option for Cheng-fu, so he changed them.

55

The orthodox Yang Cheng-fu line is held by his descendants and the students of Fu Zhong-wen, his son-in-law.

Disciples of Yang Lu-chan

Yang Lu-chan is said to have been introduced to Beijing by his students, the Wu brothers who, like Yang, came from Yongnian. Yet we know he had other personal contacts there. Initially he taught at the house of the Chang family until he came to the notice of Prince Duan who employed him as combat instructor to his Bannermen. Apart from Chen Xiu-feng whom we discussed earlier, Yang Lu-chan's famous disciples included Wu Yu-xiang (1812–80) and his elder brothers (of whom more later); Ling Shan, who was known for his striking power; Wan Chun who was known for his strength; Quan You who was known for his footwork and skill in evasion; Li Rui-dong; and Wang Lan-ting (of whom more later). Ling Shan was a Manchurian, Quan You was a Mongolian, while the others were Chinese.

Ling Shan, Quan You and Wan Chun were Bannermen, while Li Rui-dong and Wang Lan-ting were members of the household of Prince Duan, a strong supporter and even organizer of the Boxers during their rebellion of the summer of 1900. Furthermore Wang Lan-ting has a strong connection with the Tai Chi Chuan which I teach. He was forced to seek sanctuary in a Buddhist monastery after killing some Manchus, and there he taught a monk named Ching Yi (Pure One) who in turn taught Qi Min-xuan, the teacher of my own master.

Let us now move on to Yang Lu-chan's other famous students, Wu Yu-xiang and Quan You.

The Enigma of Wu Yu-xiang

Through Wu Yu-xiang's nephew, Li Yi-yu, we have writings attributed to Wu and his two elder brothers who also learned Tai Chi Chuan from Yang Lu-chan. However, Wu and his relatives do not mention Jiang Fa: why? And why does Li Yi-yu refer to his uncle's master as 'a certain Yang', yet make the absurd claim that in little over a month Wu Yu-xiang was able to learn all Chen Qing-ping's secrets at the Zhao Bao village? Why not learn at the Chen village? How did the Tai Chi Chuan classics come to be found in a salt cellar in Wuyang, where Wu Yu-xiang's brother, Cheng-ching, happened to be the local magistrate, hundreds of miles from the Wus' home in Guangping? Why does there seem to have been no contact between the Wus and the Yangs or the Chens after 1852?

The three Wu brothers from Guangping learned from Yang after he returned home from his sojourn in the Chen family village in 1850. Li says that in 1852, after Yang Lu-chan left Guangping for Beijing, Wu Yu-xiang went to visit his brother, Cheng-ching, who was magistrate of Wuyang in central Henan; *en route* he intended to learn from Chen Chang-xing, Yang's master. Instead he trained with Chen Qing-ping in the Zhao Bao village for one month, 'learning all his secrets'; in the same year, Wu Cheng-ching found the 'salt cellar' classics in Wuyang. In 1853 Chen Chang-xing died. In fact Li, writing perhaps as late as twenty-eight years after these events, is our only evidence for them; there is no other indication that Wu Yu-xiang ever got to Wuyang, or as to how his brother got the 'salt cellar classics' to him.

Was Wu persuaded not to go to the

Chen village, but to learn instead from Chen Qing-ping in the Zhao Bao village, or did Chen Chang-xing send him there because he was too old to teach Wu himself? To travel all the way to the remote Zhao Bao village which is in easy walking distance of the Chen village and yet not go on, is unbelievable. If Chen Chang-xing could not teach Wu, why did he not get his son, Keng-yun, or other students to do so?

The reason may be that Yang, teaching the elder Wu brothers when they were already in their fifties and Wu Yu-xiang when he was in his forties, did not give them a full transmission. When Yang left for Beijing, Wu decided to go to the Chen village, but Chen Chang-xing and his descendants did not want to teach a stranger who had only received a partial transmission from Yang, so Wu went to Chen Qing-ping and learned what he could of what Chen had to teach him, combining it with what he had from two years with Yang. Wu's Tai Chi Chuan is upright with high stances. The names of the techniques and the sequence are much more similar to the Yang lineage systems than the Chen, as is the method of performance. It is also comparatively rare.

Wu's main student was Li Yi-yu (1833–92), his nephew. At one point in his *Short Preface to Tai Chi Chuan*, Li wrote that the founder of Tai Chi Chuan was Chang San-feng; however, a post-script attributed to him says that the founder could never be known, but the art could only be traced to Wang Zong-yue.

Fig 24   Statue in the Chen family museum of Yang Lu-chan meeting the oncoming Chen Keng-yun's attack.

This may not be unconnected with his uncle's sojourn in the Zhao Bao village.

Li passed on the art to Hao Wei-zhen (1849–1920), and thus began Hao style which is also rare. The art then changed even further when Hao taught the *Xing Yi* and *Ba Gua* master, Sun Lu-tang (1860–1932), who combined all three arts to produce the Sun style which typically is also upright with high stances.

Some books state that Wu Yu-xiang studied with Yang Ban-hou when the latter was fifteen years of age, others have Ban-hou learning from Wu. If we look at their respective lineages, we find that there are substantial differences in the syllabus and the method of practice. Ban-hou was famous as a fighter, Wu as a writer on Tai Chi Chuan theory, and I suspect that what interchange there was, stemmed from this.

Li Yi-yu claimed that in 1852 Wu's brother found the major Tai Chi Chuan classics in Wu Yang in a salt cellar. Did anyone else have them? Did the Yangs have them from Chen Chang-xing as an oral or a written transmission? How much did Wu know? He was a student of Yang Lu-chan for only two years before Yang went to Beijing: did he *Bai Shi* with Yang? he may well not have, if Yang kept to the six year rule. Once again, an enigma.

Variations in the Yang Lineage

I will only deal here with the major schools which practise variations of the Yang styles.

Cheng Man-ching

The most famous Chinese instructor in the West, though not in the Far East, in the last thirty years is Cheng Man-ching, a student of Yang Cheng-fu and a whole lot more. Why was he so famous? First, he was the painting and calligraphy teacher of Soong Mei-ling, wife of Chiang Kai-shek, the President of Taiwan. Second, he was praised to the skies by the well-known American writer on Tai Chi Chuan, Robert W. Smith. Third, he was the first well-known teacher to come to the West to teach.

My teacher both met and pushed hands with him. He considered that Cheng Man-ching was highly cultured and that his Tai Chi was very soft; he was also of the opinion that he was not a fighter. I never met him, but I have met many of his students and I have seen him on film. My impression is also of a highly cultivated artist, but not a fighter.

Despite Cheng's protestations that he learned all he knew from Yang Cheng-fu, it is obvious that their technique was very different and we know that Cheng did train with others such as Chang Ching-ling, a student of Yang Ban-hou. Other Yang Cheng-fu lineage practitioners certainly consider that Cheng taught a different style from that practised by Yang Cheng-fu. Cheng was one of the first to popularize Tai Chi by inventing and teaching a short form.

Of Cheng's students, the only one with a reputation as a fighter is William Chen, though Robert W. Smith is wrong in claiming that Chen was a full contact champion. Many present-day practitioners of Cheng's method teach skills that Cheng never taught and probably never learned, such as spear and broadsword forms, and the Tai Chi cane form developed in the Nanjing Military Academy in the 1930s.

Tung Ying-jie

Tung was a student of Yang Cheng-fu, and

developed his own style which is popular in Europe and the USA. He was the first person in the post-war era to make a fast form popular. Tung's fast form is curious, however, because it is a combination of the fast, the slow and the still. The posture is unusual compared with other Tai Chi styles, as the back is bent over. There are techniques in the form which come from both Chen and Yang lineage systems, and some – such as Hero Stands on One Leg – which are not to be found in either. This tends to confirm that Tung did learn this form from Li Xiang-yuan of Hao style, and may account for its similarity with Zhao Bao Tai Chi.

Wang Yen-nien
Wang Yen-nien, like Cheng Man-ching, trained with Chang Ching-ling, but the form he practises is different from that of either Cheng Man-ching or practitioners of the orthodox Yang tradition. In pushing hands I have found his students to be skilful, particularly the Frenchman Serge Dreyer, though for some reason Wang, like so many, seems to have been reluctant to pass on martial knowledge.

Quan You and the other Wu Family
Quan You was a Mongolian Bannerman who underwent *Bai Shi* with Yang Ban-hou. His son, Wu Jian-chuan, adopted the Chinese surname 'Wu' (it is a different character from the 'Wu' in Wu Yu-xiang's name). Wu Jian-chuan has a high reputation as a fighter (he sought out and defeated Wan Lai-sheng after the latter had given Yang Cheng-fu a beating) and yet according to his student, Wu Tu-nan, he was defeated by the much older Song Shu-ming who turned up in Beijing around 1909. In fact it seems that a good number of masters of Tai Chi Chuan and other arts went to learn from Song, including Wu Jian-chuan and Wu Tu-nan.

This may explain why many training methods found in Wu's method, including Nine Palace and Seven Star Step, no longer exist – if they ever did in the Yang Cheng-fu line. Song taught techniques with names such as Tai Shan Angry and Push the Grinder. These names do not occur in Wu or Yang schools, though the technique described may exist, but under a different name.

The third generation of the Wu family included Wu's two sons, of whom Wu Kung-yi was the more famous for his brief and inconclusive fight in Macau in 1954 with the White Crane Master Chan Hak-fu. Wu must be praised for his bravery because Chan was more than twenty years younger than him. However, in the book *Wu Family Tai Chi Chuan* by his brother, Wu Kung-Zao, we can compare Kung-yi's technique to his father. The comparison is far from favourable to the son, and the technique is very different. I will discuss this book later.

In the 1980s, Wu Jian-chuan's son-in-law, Ma Yue-liang, announced that there was a Wu family fast form: but this is the first the Tai Chi world had heard of it. So what is Wu style, and what is not? My teacher's uncle, Cheng Wing-kwong, learned from Wu Jian-chuan in Hong Kong, but also from others. There are many students of Wu Jian-chuan who have good form and good pushing hands; yet since the time of Wu Kung-yi, none from later generations has proved himself as a fighter. I can only surmise that this was because he kept, or tried to keep things within the family. Indeed, the Ma Yue-liang branch no longer teach the twenty-four *Nei Kung* exercises, if they ever did.

Qi Min-xuan

Qi was not a famous master, mainly because he was not a professional martial artist and because he had only one long-term student, rather than because of a lack of ability; so it is ironic that this outsider is responsible for an explosion of martial Tai Chi Chuan in both the West and the Far East. Qi's father was a student of Quan You, the first generation of the Wu family, so he was introduced to quality Tai Chi Chuan at an early age. His main master, however, was an obscure Buddhist monk named Ching Yi (the Pure One). We do not know Ching Yi's real name or much else about him, except that he learned the art from Wang Lan-ting.

Wang is the only person I'm aware of who trained with both Chen Keng-yun, son of Chen Chang-xing, and with Yang Lu-chan. Based on the data available, this must have been between the mid-1850s and 1870 – which makes it very curious, because if *he* could learn Tai Chi from Chen Chang-xing's son, then why couldn't Wu Yu-xiang also? It makes me suspect that they didn't want to teach Wu, who was only willing or able to stay for a short time, and who had already trained with Yang Lu-chan; and so Wu sought out the only available alternative, Chen Qing-ping.

Qi Min-xuan's twenty-four exercise, *Nei Kung* method which he'd learned from Ching Yi was almost identical with that of the Wu family at the time of Wu Jian-chuan. The fact that the Yangs do not teach this method today suggests that it was something rarely taught to outsiders by the Yang family. Wu Jian-chuan continued this tradition and only had three disciples in his time in Hong Kong, one of whom was Cheng Wing-kwong, the uncle of my teacher. Wing-kwong did not, however, complete the course of training in *Nei Kung*.

Qi's method continues today in both Hong Kong and the West where I and other students of Cheng Tin-hung have helped in spreading it to many countries. We are now also part of the history.

MY OWN TAI CHI CHUAN

The Tai Chi that I teach is Chen style, Yang style, Wang style, Wu style, Ching Yi style, Qi style, Cheng style and Docherty style because people with these different names and others before them have all played a part in its transmission. I teach Tai Chi Chuan so that people in many countries can use it for self defence as well as for improving their health, for that reason I call my art Practical Tai Chi Chuan International. When asked what style of Tai Chi Chuan I teach, my reply is 'Wudang'.

4 Inside the Door

We have already discussed the concept of *Men Ren* or Door Person – students who have been shown inside-the-door techniques after undergoing ritual initiation. Let us now look at what this involves.

RITUAL INITIATION

One reason that Tai Chi Chuan is referred to as an internal martial art is because of the concepts of 'inside the door' tuition and *Zhen Chuan* which comes with *Bai Shi*. The character for '*Bai*' symbolizes two hands held down together, and this is the pose adopted by the Chinese when showing respect or reverence to the gods, or to a superior in status such as a teacher; by extension it can mean 'to worship'.

In Cantonese '*Sifu*' is the formal term of address for an instructor of the Chinese martial arts or a skilled practitioner of any discipline. The Mandarin term is '*Shi Fu*': the character '*Shi*' is a drawing of one (the first) banner that stayed at the capital and by extension meant the 'one above the others' and thus the commander-in-chief, master, or suchlike. The same character is used in the term *Baishi*.

There are two different characters which can be used for '*Fu*' in the context

Fig. 26   Shi.

Fig. 25   Bai.

Fig 27   The second character for 'Fu', meaning 'father'.

61

of *Shi Fu/Sifu*: the first means 'one who acts' or 'arranges', that is, a teacher or instructor; the second means 'father', and is composed of a hand and a stick or axe – the father was considered the chief and the instructor of his family. Another term used for teacher is '*Lao Shi*': again, it is the same character for *Shi*, while *Lao* means old: – in traditional Chinese society the old were revered for their experience and knowledge. Since the Revolution, the Chinese government in its attack on 'feudalism' has discouraged the use of these terms, and encouraged use of the term '*Jiao Lian*' meaning coach or trainer.

Why the opposition to the traditional teaching method? Why do most practitioners of Chinese martial arts in the West know nothing of *Bai Shi*? Why is it not more widely practised? What is its purpose? Is it still relevant in modern society?

Let us consider the cultural context out of which *Bai Shi* came. First, every society sooner or later becomes hierarchical; with the influence of Confucianism and its concept of filial piety, or respect for one's elders, Chinese society is particularly prone to this. Second, there is the long and sometimes uneasy relationship which Chinese martial arts have had with Chinese religion and philosophy; this has led to the adoption of certain ritualistic, meditative and philosophical elements into martial arts practice. The use of the character *Bai* emphasizes this.

BAI SHI

In the context of Tai Chi Chuan, *Bai Shi* is a ceremony with ritual elements conducted by a master in which students 'enter the door' and become disciples. After the conditions of *Bai Shi* have been made clear to the students, they agree to accept them and the ceremony begins. Normally this would be at the master's home or studio where there is a portrait of Chang San-feng. Usually there is a fee paid by the student, traditionally in a red packet as red is a propitious colour and it is considered indelicate to display money openly. The master then places an offering of fruit in front of the founder's portrait, and lights a ritual number of incense sticks; these he gives to the student who kneels down before a portrait and gives the *koutou* (knocks the head) three times to show his respect to the founder's memory. The student then faces the master and again gives the *koutou*, after which the incense is placed in an incense burner in front of the portrait. The ceremony is over: the student has entered the door.

So what are the implications of the ceremony? By undergoing *Bai Shi* a student has made a commitment to the school, to the founder, and to his kung fu brothers and sisters as well as to his master. In return the master allows the student to enter the door and to receive a true transmission of the art (*Zhen Chuan*) including *Nei Kung*. The student can now be referred to as *Men Ren* – or literally, 'door person' – and is regarded as a disciple of the master and no longer as a mere student.

This type of initiation ritual is mirrored in Chinese secret societies, and in Buddhist and Taoist religious orders. In all of these groups the initiation ceremony was only the first step in a long process of transmitting the inner teachings to a disciple, a process which could take decades. The process was designed to produce a band of brothers (sisters in the case of nunneries) who could recognize one another as such by special jargon or knowledge of certain techniques.

The desire for freedom from an oppressive government is expressed in the phrase 'mountains high, emperor far', meaning that in a remote place there was less chance of government interference. This led to martial arts being practised in monasteries and temples in the mountains, places such as Er Mei Shan and Wudang Shan. It is not surprising that *Bai Shi* grew up in this type of environment.

It used to be that students of Tai Chi Chuan underwent *Bai Shi* at a very early stage and were taught *Nei Kung* first. This changed as Tai Chi Chuan began to be taught commercially and the form was taught first; and so it came to pass that the form was all that most people ever learned, and all that most people were able to teach. Later masters adopted the rule that students had to visit the master for three years, and then the master had to visit the student for three years; then if the student showed sincerity and commitment, he would be accepted for initiation. If these rules were rigidly applied, many people in fact never went through *Bai Shi*.

In 1995 when I visited my teacher in Zhongshan, I met a doctor from Shanghai who had trained for many years with Ma Yue-liang and Wu Ying-hua, the daughter of the great master Wu Jian-chuan. He told me that he had come from Shanghai in the hope of undergoing *Bai Shi* with my teacher, as Ma Yue-liang and Wu Ying-hua were unable or unwilling to teach the twenty-four Tai Chi *Nei Kung* exercises. In fact Cheng Wing-kwong, my teacher's uncle, was one of only three people to undergo *Bai Shi* with Wu Jian-chuan in Hong Kong, and even then he was not taught all the exercises.

Why is it that great masters such as Wu Jian-chuan gave *Bai Shi* to so few students? I believe that part of the reason was to keep it within the family, partly also so that there would not be competition.

Many teachers in the Far East abuse *Bai Shi*. The British martial arts writer, Nigel Sutton, told me of a famous (now deceased) Cheng Man-ching style master who charged a lot of money for *Bai Shi*, but taught nothing in return; people were in fact paying to have their names recorded as disciples. Further, often students claim to have trained with a master, or even to be an 'inside-the-door' student, when at best they have only a nodding acquaintance with him. And often masters of one style will also train with masters of another style, but will not acknowledge the latter as their master. For example in the early seventies the chief European representative of Yang-style Tai Chi Chuan spent some weeks training in *San Shou* and pushing hands with my teacher in Hong Kong.

Other masters, particularly when they get old, have students do the *Bai Shi* ceremony with them, but then do not teach them personally, delegating the task to a senior student. So, many people who have learned *Nei Kung* or other 'inside-the-door' training after *Bai Shi* have not actually had it at first hand from a master.

It was only in 1995 on a trip to China that I felt how it was to train Tai Chi Chuan in the days before Yang Lu-chan brought the art to Beijing. In 1984 I had visited Wudang Mountain where Chang San-feng had lived for some years, but following my reading of *Researches into Tai Chi Chuan* which is based on the work and experiences of the late Wu Tu-nan, I went to Bao Ji and the Chen family village, both of which Wu had visited in 1917.

Bao Ji is in Shaanxi province, about three hours by train from the ancient capital of Xian, and Chang San-feng lived there in the Taoist Temple of the Golden Pavilion. It was there that Wang Zong or Wang Zong-yue was said by Wu to have trained in *Nei Jia Chuan* or Tai Chi Chuan which had been passed down from the time of Chang San-feng. Thus the art was truly taught 'inside the door' – that is, in an enclosed religious community – and this goes a long way to explain the ritual ceremony and the use of incense sticks. Further, in the Chen family village, standing outside the large wooden doors of the house where Yang Lu-chan was taught by Chen Chang-xing, you can see nothing of what is going on inside. I believe that the training was done here, rather than in an open area, so that practitioners of the Chen family *Pao Chui* (Cannon Punch) method could not see the Tai Chi training. Again, inside the door.

Fig 28 View of the Golden Pavilion Temple in Bao Ji.

Historically I believe that Tai Chi training was only done in very small groups so the teacher and students knew one another intimately. The more recent rule of waiting for six years before being able to start learning 'inside-the-door' training is one that my teacher refused to follow. He started teaching Tai Chi Chuan professionally in 1949 in a Hong Kong where there were famous teachers of the Yang and Wu families. People went to him for two reasons: because he could teach the art in a practical way; and because they could learn quickly. This led to a delegation of older masters beating a path to his door to ask him to follow the six-year rule before giving *Bai Shi* to a student. He agreed to stop, but only if they took over the upkeep of his family. They refused.

We have dealt in some detail with who can receive *Bai Shi*, but who can give it? Normally only when a master has given formal permission can a student give *Bai Shi*. Unfortunately there are loose cannons in the Tai Chi world who want to be seen as great masters, who have learned certain of the 'inside-the-door' aspects, but who lack the knowledge and ability to give true transmission.

I know a Chinese teacher of Tai Chi Chuan who trained both with my teacher and his uncle. He is a large gentleman and is renowned for his ability to take punches to the stomach; he has had no correction since the 1950s. A master of Yang-style Tai Chi from California wanted to undergo *Bai Shi* and learn *Nei Kung* from our friend. Our friend charged him a lot of money. The Yang master, believing that he now had *Nei Kung*, then tried a demonstration which is done in my teacher's school, of having a student jump onto his stomach from a height of six feet.

My teacher received a phone call from the said Yang stylist who was bleeding from the rectum as well as coughing up and urinating blood. On hearing who the poor chap had learned from, my teacher told him it was hardly surprising and sent him to learn anew from one of his old students who worked as a rubbish collector in Chinatown. This cured him. In Tai Chi Chuan, in *Bai Shi*, as in life, the rule is: *caveat emptor.*

Zhen Chuan: True Transmission

We don't train just for our own sakes, but so that we can develop sufficiently to pass on what the Chinese term '*Zhen Chuan*', or true transmission. The character '*Zhen*' has a special connotation, and a '*Zhen Ren*' is one who has transformed himself in the eyes of others through Taoistic practice. Only a Zhen Ren is capable of *Zhen Chuan*, which can be written or oral.

ORAL TRANSMISSION

'Oral transmission and development by the mind' refers to private tuition of key concepts and techniques which the student is then left to develop; this is what makes Tai Chi Chuan such a complex art. *The Six Secret Words of Tai Chi Chuan* are an example of oral *Zhen Chuan*. They are also six practical concepts which can be applied to techniques in different combinations to render them more effective, especially in the field of attacking vital points. However, they are almost useless to anyone who does not have a foundation in the art.

There are also inner techniques (techniques within techniques) which are not actually given a separate name when the form is taught in an open class, but which do have a name and application for inside-the-door students (see the section on long form). And there are variations: for example, many Tai Chi Chuan teachers are aware of the concept of *Cai Lang* or The Uprooting Wave, but few are aware of the different variations.

All this amounts to a great problem for those wishing to acquire a complete knowledge of the Tai Chi Chuan syllabus, as few teachers have such knowledge, and even fewer are willing to pass it on to more than a handful of people.

WRITTEN TRANSMISSION

There are two types of written transmission: primary and secondary, the primary sources being the Tai Chi Chuan classics. Where did they come from ? We cannot be certain: many phrases in them are taken from other works on philosophy, poetry, history, military strategy and Taoist alchemy. Some of the material in them is to be found in *Nei Jia Chuan* writings predating Yang Lu-chan's arrival in Beijing in 1852 and some can be found in works on *Ba Gua* and *Xing Yi* boxing.

The Tai Chi Chuan Classics

What are the Tai Chi Chuan classics ? There are dozens of texts purporting to be classics. My teacher recounts that his master gave him a copy of five texts said to be such and made him learn them by heart and chant them when practising *Nei Kung*. This accounts for their mnemonic nature – two of them are actually called '*Ge*', meaning 'songs'; it also accounts for the great variety in content between one version of a text and another. Let us discuss them in turn.

First there is the *Tai Chi Chuan Lun* which has been attributed both to Chang San-feng and to Wang Zong-yue. 'Lun' means 'discourse' or 'analects', and was the name given to the collected sayings of Confucius. The text discusses posture, internal alchemy and fighting; it also mentions the phrase *Shi San Shi* or Thirteen Tactics, linking these to the Eight Trigrams and to the Five Elements.

Second, there is the *Tai Chi Chuan Ching*. The term '*Ching*' means 'classic' or 'book' or 'canon', and so we have the *I Ching* or *Classic of Change* and the *Tao Te Ching* or *Classic of The Way and Virtue*. Indeed, the latter two works are quoted in the text which contains strong philosophical and cosmological elements and starts off as an almost word-for-word quotation of Zhou Dun-yi's explanation of the Tai Chi symbol. There is a brief reference to sinking the Qi to the *Tan Tien*, but the rest of the essay talks about the strategies and tactics to be adopted when fighting.

Third, there is the *Shi San Shi Xing Gong Xin Jue*. I translate this as *Imagining the Use of theThirteen Tactics*. Although the title mentions the Thirteen Tactics, the essay does not: it begins by discussing the connection between mind, movement and the circulation of *Qi*, which is also alluded to later in the text. It talks about the appearance being like an eagle seizing a rabbit, and the spirit like a cat taking a mouse. It emphasizes distinguishing full and empty, moving like a great river, and being still as a sacred mountain. It discusses *Jin*, or 'force', and the connection between hardness and softness. It draws the comparison of the mind being the commander of an army using the *Qi* and the waist to send orders.

Tacked on to this text is another essay which begins 'It is also said...'. This lends support to my view that these texts are a collection of sayings designed to be recited. For the most part this addendum goes over points already made in the main text, but tells us that the body and intent should be completely on the *Jing Shen* and not on the Qi, or there will be no strength. This has led to a lot of confusion in Tai Chi circles about how to breathe, which we will discuss later.

The fourth text is the *Shi San Shi Ge*, or *The Song of the Thirteen Tactics*. Again, although the Thirteen Tactics are mentioned in the title, they are not named in the text, which stresses the use of the intent in moving, turning and changing. The martial aspects in this text are less explicit. The song states, 'To enter the door and be led along the path, oral transmission is necessary', a clear reference to *Bai Shi*.

The final text is the *Da Shou Ge* or *Hit Hands Song*. This text is often wrongly translated as the *Song of Pushing Hands*, but it is clearly about fighting and a more accurate translation would be *The Fighters' Song*. It discusses key concepts such as following, using 4oz of force to displace 1,000lb, and leading the opponent into emptiness. It also has an addendum which begins, 'Finally it is said...': this gives six groups of three characters and concludes with four characters, all containing practical advice about fighting. This will be addressed later.

Other Tai Chi Chuan Writings

There have been suggestions that Yang Lu-chan and possibly his sons were illiterate, as we don't know of any writings in their hand and there is no record of their having passed any examinations. However, the same could be said of many martial artists of their time; my teacher, for example, has never passed any examinations either, but has written four books on Tai Chi Chuan.

Yang Lu-chan's student Wu Yu-xiang has been credited with writing a number of Tai Chi Chuan texts, including one, the title of which is often translated as *The Five Word Secret*, although there are more than five words and none of them is secret. In the 1996 *Lost T'ai-chi Classics from the Late Ching Dynasty* by Professor Douglas Wile, we have texts which purport to be written by Wu Yu-xiang's elder brothers and by his nephew Li Yi-yu, published in China in 1993. The professor has done a service to the Tai Chi Chuan community by writing his book, but we have insufficient information to prove the authenticity of these texts — there are inevitably problems with such material. For example, according to the professor, one of the Wu brothers, Wu Cheng-ching, 'introduces a theory ... that appears nowhere in the received classics or anywhere else I am aware of.' This refers to a passage about taking advantage of the moment when the old *Jin* or force — the professor translates *Jin* as 'energy' — has passed, and the new energy has not issued to hit the opponent. The professor also gives only an eight-line version of *The Fighters' Song*.

Cheng Tin-hung, in two of his books on Tai Chi Chuan, gives a ten-line version of the song containing some of Wu's eight lines. My teacher's version from Qi Min-xuan states, 'Lead the opponent into emptiness and immediately discharge (ie counter-attack)'. Wu does quote this saying in another text, but Professor Wile fails to connect it with Wu's 'new theory'.

Two centuries before Wu, the great Japanese swordsman Miyamoto Musashi had the same concept, which he called 'hitting the enemy in one timing'. The lost Wu texts are of academic value, but they don't in fact take our understanding of Tai Chi Chuan much further.

In 1980 Wu Jian-chuan's descendants reprinted a book by Wu Gong-Zao; it included photos of a handwritten book which purported to have been in their family for over a hundred years and to have been given to Wu Quan-you by Yang Ban-hou. Professor Wile has transcribed and translated these texts in his book also.

The list of contents to these texts, which may be in the same hand, only lists the names of thirty-two of the texts, omitting the last eight. The last three of the texts are attributed to Chang San-feng and are concerned with internal alchemy. The thirty-ninth text seems to approve of sexual congress with male and female pre-pubescent youths, and for that reason alone I believe these last three texts at least to be spurious, and condemned them in issue no 46 of *Fighting Arts International Magazine* in 1988. They have no place in Tai Chi Chuan written transmissions, and are of academic interest only.

The other texts in the collection are of interest as, apart from the names of certain techniques, they are the first direct references to attacking vital points in Tai Chi Chuan literature.

CHI KUNG (QI GONG) AND NEI KUNG

It is said that 'Training *Chuan* without training *Kung*, even if done until old age, is still in vain.' In other words, some type of martial *Nei/Qi Kung/Gong*

Fig 29   Demonstration of Tai Chi Nei Kung by the author.

conditioning training is necessary if we wish to be able to fight. This statement is as true for internal martial arts as it is for external ones. Tai Chi Chuan, perhaps uniquely, combines martial, meditative, therapeutic, religious and philosophical qualities. One would therefore expect *Tai Chi Kung* to possess these qualities. Unfortunately most of the systems being taught or demonstrated under the title '*Tai Chi Qi Gong* /*Tai Chi Nei Kung*', while they may fit some of these requirements, are distinctly lacking in martial qualities, so each type of *Kung* must be analysed and empirically tested before it can be declared to fit our requirements.

It is my contention that it is a search for this very martial quality that has led to the development of sudden '*Fa Jin*' movements within hand forms, to the development of fast forms, and to Tai Chi practitioners dabbling in so-called 'harder' styles to give them the *Kung* training which their own system lacks. Clearly when he taught Tai Chi Chuan to the Imperial Guard, Yang Lu-chan had some effective *Kung* method. However, after the overthrow of the Ching dynasty and the sudden growth in popularity of Tai Chi Chuan, it would seem that some members of famous Tai Chi families either did not, or could not, pass on an effective *Kung* method to their students.

I took up Tai Chi Chuan with my

master, Cheng Tin-hung, because his Tai Chi was lively and stylish and both he and his students had fought with considerable success in full contact contests against hard-style kung fu practitioners all over south-east Asia. Their success in these contests was to some extent due to strategy and tactics, but was more directly attributable to effective *Kung* training. The most important aspect of *Kung* training lay in the twenty-four *Tai Chi Nei Kung* methods which he taught.

Twenty-four Technique *Tai Chi Nei Kung*

As these techniques are part of the inner art, they are beyond the scope of this book and I will discuss them rather than show them. There are twelve Yin and twelve Yang exercises. Ideally, we would do the twelve Yin exercises and the last Yang exercise one day and the twelve Yang exercises and the first Yin exercise the next day, and continue to alternate them – although if you are sick or feeling weak, then it is better to place more emphasis on the Yin exercises. This gives us a daily training regimen of Thirteen Tactics, all of which in different combinations are trained in the *Nei Kung*.

Some exercises are static and have no direct self-defence purpose, although they are very useful in strengthening the joints and tendons and training the determination; others are moving and have one or more applications as well as some therapeutic aspect. Only the third part of the final Yang exercise contains a purely meditative aspect. The therapeutic aspects make the body more flexible and hence less prone to injury, and are also useful as a type of self-administered physiotherapy

to help with joint, tendon and bone injuries.

The exercises can be done on three levels: the basic level for all the exercises would take up to one hour for either the Yin or the Yang set; the intermediate level for Tai Chi fighters takes from two to three hours; while the advanced level for Tai Chi masters could take up to seven hours. The exercises are also referred to as one hundred-day *Kung*: after daily practice of the Yin exercises for this period as well as abstinence from sex, male students can be tested by taking blows to the body and having someone jump onto the abdomen from a height of six feet.

I strongly recommend that those interested in *Nei Kung/Qi Gong* training of any type should be extremely careful in their choice of teacher and in the type of *Nei Kung/Qi Gong* which they choose.

It is possible with certain methods to acquire valuable martial abilities, but the cost in terms of side effects can involve impotence, arthritis and psychological problems. I personally know people in Hong Kong who have suffered nervous breakdowns as a result of certain *Qi Gong* training. In this type of training we are dealing with the respiratory system, circulation, the nervous system and the brain, so any imbalance in the training is bound to be reflected in the balance of energies in the body and mind of the practitioner. I'll discuss this in more detail later.

If you do encounter problems, stop the training and consult your teacher in the first instance; if the problems persist, stop the training and find another teacher. The twenty-four Tai Chi *Nei Kung* exercises are a marvellous method of exercise if practiced properly. I do from four to twenty-four of these exercises every day.

Fig 30   Sifu Cheng Kam demonstrating Tai Chi Nei Kung in Hong Kong.

If I have to choose, I'd do these exercises rather than practise the hand form. They are that important. Each individual exercise can be practised on three levels: student, adept and master. It can take anything from fifty minutes to seven hours to practice twelve exercises.

This kind of training regimen, over and above the other aspects of the art, is physically demanding and time-consuming even at the basic level, and this is another reason why so few people ever learn or are able to teach a complete system of Tai Chi Chuan.

5 Hand Form

All Tai Chi methods have a hand form, or series of interconnected, flowing martial techniques performed slowly. However, although there are hundreds of different forms, most are derived from one origin, as the long forms of famous masters such as Wu Jian-chuan, Yang Cheng-fu and Wu Yu-xiang follow the same basic sequence, though with certain deviations and technical differences in execution.

My teacher teaches a long form which takes from fifteen to thirty minutes to complete; it is similar to that taught by Wu Jian-chuan, but contains certain additional techniques. First of all he teaches the techniques square, that is, broken down into simplified movements; this can be compared to school children being taught block letters before they are shown joined-up writing. Thus square form is a teaching tool rather than an end in itself. He then teaches the student to make the techniques flow, and this is known as round form; this is real Tai Chi Chuan.

Square form is easy for the student to follow, and it is easy for the teacher to make corrections. It clearly defines each separate technique so the student will remember its name and sequence more readily, and it is particularly useful in teaching correct stance, posture, focus and co-ordination. Round form is something of a misnomer, as Tai Chi does contain some straight line movement; even so, the essence of Tai Chi Chuan is circle and focus.

The gentle bending, twisting, contracting and extending movements of the round form, combined with deep harmonious breathing, provide an excellent tonic and massage for the muscles, tendons, joints, organs, nervous system and circulation. The main martial purpose of the round form is to educate the body in relaxing, in efficient movement and in the use of total body force. The form can also be done in mirror image, but while this is useful training, it is not essential for the average student. For the really keen, the form can be done in reverse or even mirror image in reverse.

In recent years many teachers, myself included, have started to teach 'short forms'; these have many of the techniques of the traditional forms but with most of the repetitions removed. In the West, due to reasons of climate and lifestyle, most teachers are unable to teach every day and most students are unable to train every day, so that learning a traditional form could, for some students, take over a year. In my opinion short forms are not as efficacious as the traditional forms, but they are a necessary innovation and should be used as a stepping stone towards learning the traditional forms.

Almost every student and teacher of Tai Chi Chuan sincerely believes that the particular form which they practise is the original and best, the same as that practised by the great masters of the past such as Yang Lu-chan. Yet there is a tremendous variation in style, in technique, in content and in attitude.

TEN CRITERIA TO IMPROVE FORM

In 1991, after a visit to the Far East, I introduced Tai Chi forms competitions to Britain. In Tai Chi Chuan, whatever the style, we all subscribe to certain basic principles – at least in theory. Based on these principles, I devised ten criteria which could be used to judge these competitions; I have also found them to be a useful way of improving both my own form and that of my students. Moreover the Dutch Tai Chi Federation and other instructors have endorsed these same principles by using them for their competitions. I will explain these criteria to you in the hope that whether you are a teacher or a student, you can use them in your daily 6 a.m. practice.

Correct Posture

The first is correctness of posture. This is controversial: in the *Song of the Thirteen Tactics* we learn that 'when the coccyx is *Zhong Zheng*, the Spirit connects with the headtop'. What is *Zhong Zheng*? And how does the spirit 'connect with the headtop'?

Zhong literally means central; *Zheng* can mean straight, upright or correct. There are Tai Chi fascists who insist that the back should be upright/erect – yet we have pictures of many famous masters such as Yang Cheng-fu, Chen Wei-ming, Tung Ying-jie and Sun Lu-tang, all of whom can be seen with a straight, but not an upright back. Essentially it was Cheng Man-ching who practised with an upright back, and it is interesting to compare his postures with those of Yang Cheng-fu who seems to have been his main teacher. The late Huang Jifu, who knew Cheng, rightly described him as a man of mystery. Who taught him to practise in an upright posture? Was it his own idea? Why do it?

Now, if practitioners of other schools practise with an upright back, that's fine and their form should be assessed on that basis. Equally, if people practise with a straight but not always upright back, they should be assessed on that basis. Beyond this, however, leaning and tilting the body are generally to be avoided.

The idea behind all this is that if the back is straight (whether or not it is also upright) the lungs can expand comfortably and take in an optimal amount of oxygen: bad posture leads to poor respiration which leads to poor circulation. Furthermore when the back is straight, the spine is correctly aligned, thus enhancing the function of the central nervous system which runs through the spinal cord.

Correctness of Stance

The second criteria is correctness of stance: alignment of the knee and foot is crucial here. Incorrect alignment – due in part to poor instruction – has led to many people having to give up martial arts.

Front Stance
In a front stance, both feet should be flat

on the ground. The front knee should be bent directly over the toes, but without going way past them. The rear foot should generally be pointing forward, and particularly so when the next move involves stepping back, as failure to do so results in poor balance and affects the posture. The length of the stance varies, depending on the technique. Usually when stepping back into a front stance, the stance will be longer, as in Step Back to Beat the Tiger. The width of the stance should be that of the shoulders. (Weight distribution will be discussed later.)

Back Stance

The back stance is more difficult, and there are widespread variations depending on the technique and Tai Chi style. The knee of the rear leg should be bent directly over, but not much beyond the toes of the back foot. The rear foot does not always face in exactly the same direction as the front foot, as in Seven Stars Style, but for balance and to protect the joint the rear foot is normally turned in so that it makes an approximate 45-degree angle with the front foot. Sometimes in variations of the back stance such as the cat stance, both feet are close together, but usually when a back stance precedes a front stance, the feet should be a shoulder-width apart and at least that in length between the heel of the front foot and the toes of the rear foot.

Particularly in long back stances such as Snake Creeps Down, the knee joint of the rear leg is under tremendous pressure, so do be very careful to ensure correct alignment or your snake will find creeping down increasingly painful.

Horse-Riding Stance

The horse-riding stance is the subject of a great deal of misunderstanding. Performed correctly, it is superb in building powerful leg muscles, stretching the tendons, strengthening the knee joints and stimulating the circulation in the groin area. Most important is that the feet should not be parallel: if they are, you will not be able to sink into the stance properly, and will end up pushing the knees forwards and beyond the toes, a position which in time will badly damage the knee joints. I have taught many students who had damaged their knees in this way when practising other systems.

The feet should be turned out between about 20–45 degrees. The weight should be kept on the heel and the outside of the foot, and should be evenly distributed (nb. this is not an example of what is termed double-weightedness, a concept which I will define and explain later). You should sink into the stance so that ideally the thighs are almost parallel to the ground in order to stretch the tendons and stimulate the autonomic nervous system. Older persons and beginners will find it difficult to sink so far at first, but as the joints become looser and they learn to relax it will become easier. On no account should you force yourself into this position.

In both kicks and normal standing posture as in Cross Hands, the weight should neither be forward nor back. Again, I should emphasize that the standing posture is not an example of double-weightedness.

Footwear

While we are talking about stance, a word on footwear. I don't wear *kung fu* slippers for two reasons: first, more than twenty years of martial arts training, including nine years in the Hong Kong Police, has given me big feet. Second, one of my Tai Chi elder brothers told me that he preferred to wear trainers because if he had to kick someone they gave more protection to his feet. If you do choose to wear trainers, use ones with a firm sole and not those of the jogging type which are more difficult to balance on. However, there is no doubt that for demonstration purposes kung fu slippers look more elegant and are much lighter on the feet, a factor worth considering when doing a long form which can take more than fifteen minutes to complete.

Distinguishing Yin and Yang

Next to consider is distinguishing Yin and Yang. Alternatively we can eschew Chinese terminology and talk about distinguishing the substantial and the void, or the full and the empty.

This concept can be appreciated most clearly when considering weight distribution. For example, in a front stance the front leg bears most of the weight and is therefore full, substantial or Yin, while the rear leg is empty, void or Yang; whereas in a back stance, the front leg is empty, void or Yang while the rear leg is full, substantial or Yin. It seems simple, but remember it is Tai Chi Chuan that we are talking about. First of all, people often ask why the front leg in a front stance or the back leg in a back stance should be Yin, when in each case the said leg is full, substantial and strong? Likewise how can the rear leg in a front stance or the front leg in a back stance be Yang, when in each case the said leg is also empty and void?

To ask such questions indicates a limited understanding of Yin and Yang. Yang is the positive force and represents movement; Yin is the negative force and repre-

sents stillness. In a front stance, if the weight is properly distributed it should be possible to take a step with the rear leg without first shifting the weight forward, while it should be impossible to step with the front foot without first shifting the weight back. Because the rear leg has the immediate potential for movement, it is Yang and because the front leg does not possess this capacity, it is Yin.

In a back stance for the same reason, the front leg is Yang while the rear leg is Yin. No doubt some of you have by now concluded that in the horse-riding stance both legs are Yin, and that as the weight is equally distributed, this is also an example of the deadly Tai Chi sin of double-weightedness. Certainly both legs in a horse-riding stance are Yin – however, this is not double-weightedness. The *Tai Chi Chuan Ching* (*Classic of Tai Chi Chuan*) tells us that if we wish to be free of the sickness of double-weightedness, we must know Yin and Yang. The corollary is that if there is no Yin and Yang, there is double-weightedness. In a horse-riding stance, if there is the *Zhong Zheng* that I referred to earlier, then the upper body will possess the capacity for movement and provide the Yang to complement the Yin of the legs.

Distinguishing Yin and Yang is also done in other ways, such as opening and closing, contracting and expanding. For example, the technique Twist the Body and Kick involves an expansive upward movement of the arms which opens the ribcage, followed by a contracting downward movement of the arms which closes the ribcage. Another example is Brush Knee Twist Step, where the striking hand is cupped and then straightened and expanded as it strikes.

Finally, although Yin and Yang must be

distinguished, nevertheless there should be an element of Yin in the Yang and vice versa as the Tai Chi symbol shows. In other words, extremes are to be avoided, so that for example when we straighten the arm in order to push or punch, we should avoid locking the joint.

Co-ordinated Movement

The next criterion is co-ordinated movement. This is one of the more difficult goals for beginners to achieve, partly because Tai Chi is very deceptive: it seems as if it is the arms that are moving most of the time, although this is not so; there is minimal independent arm movement in Tai Chi Chuan. The *Tai Chi Chuan Discourse* (*Lun*) puts it well:

> The root is in the feet,
> It is discharged via the legs,
> Is controlled by the waist
> and takes shape in the fingers.
> From the feet, to the legs, to the waist,
> All must be completely uniform and simultaneous,
> Whether moving forward or back,
> This will result in good timing and correct movement

The aim is for all parts of the body to start and finish a movement together – and yet many Tai Chi practitioners fail to do this. I believe that a major cause of this is that many practitioners do not know how to practise pushing hands drills, *Nei Kung* and self-defence applications – or if they do, they fail to do so. All these three aspects require the use of total body force, and all are easier to learn than the form. This is why I teach beginners pushing hands and self defence from the first class which they attend.

The importance of this was brought home to me in Hong Kong back in 1989 when I was with my teacher watching a teacher training class on his rooftop studio in Kowloon. The lady taking the class seemed oblivious to the fact that in techniques such as Parry and Punch, and Brush Knee Twist Step where there is a forward-directed punch or strike, a majority of her charges were letting their bodyweight come forward over their front feet before they had delivered the particular strike or technique, instead of having the weight behind the technique.

For all I know they are still doing the form, and even teaching it in the same way. In their classes only the form and perhaps the sword are taught, so they and their students are not aware of the implications of their poor technique. From a martial point of view it would be like stepping towards the opponent into a stance and then punching him, instead of releasing the punch as you step forward. This convinced me that those who practise the form alone have no hope of attaining a high level of ability in Tai Chi Chuan.

A few years ago I taught the traditional long form to a class at the Bank of China in London. Most of the students were not so interested in self defence, but I taught them pushing hands and a few basic applications to improve their co-ordination. The advantage of pushing hands drills is that the same basic movements are repeated again and again, unlike the form techniques which are infinitely variable and complex; thus the simpler techniques of pushing hands help to improve the co-ordination, which in turn makes it easier for the students to learn the more complex form movements.

Often students find it difficult to sink into stances when practising the form. This can best be remedied by Nei Kung training, where there is a heavy emphasis on both sinking and turning the body as a technique is applied; a further advantage is that each exercise is repeated many times.

There are other essential types of co-ordination such as mental and physical, soft and hard, internal and external, stillness and motion. To sum up, if there is no co-ordination then there is no technique; and with no technique, there is no power.

Achieving Smoothness, Intent and Focus

The next two criteria to consider are opposites yet in a way complementary. On the one hand, Tai Chi practitioners should seek to achieve a smooth transition from one technique to another, but on the other hand their techniques should exhibit both intent and focus. This is not easy to achieve.

In my own style we have square form and round form. Square form was invented in the 1920s when Wu Jian-quan was teaching Tai Chi Chuan at Beijing University. Because of the large number of people in the classes, many students could not see clearly or identify certain of the individual techniques in the hand form. The solution was first, to break down the individual techniques. Second, a count of one, two, three was used to divide each technique into component parts which were as far as possible a multiple of three. Three is a significant number in Taoist numerology and cosmology in that it symbolizes the unity of heaven, earth and humanity and therefore perfection and completion. Because of the linear nature of this form it was called square form, as opposed to the spiralling movements of what then came to be referred to as the round form.

Through practising the square form, each posture could be held for seconds or minutes so that the teacher could walk round correcting students; and the students themselves had a clearer idea of the individual techniques and the correct appellation of each move. The square form also enabled students to achieve better focus as the teacher would correct the body alignment of each student.

In Wing Chun, much is made of centre line theory; but this theory is not the sole property of the practitioners of Sticking Hands and Butterfly Swords. In Tai Chi Chuan the knee of the forward leg, the nose and the hand(s) should all be aligned in the same direction when striking, kicking or pushing. This is correct focus, and when it is achieved the whole weight of the body is behind the strike, kick or push. A Tai Chi practitioner, and indeed any martial artist lacking this focus can only be considered a beginner.

Intent is something else: intent, or *Yi*, is constantly referred to in the Tai Chi classics. So how do we identify it, what is its precise meaning, and why is it so important?

We should be able to see the *Yi* expressed not just through the physical movements, but also in the eyes. Students often ask where they should be looking when practising the form, and to start with, many teachers tell them to look at the hands; however; this is not quite right. Rather than looking at the hands, they should be looking at where they, and therefore their hands are going. At all times the hands and feet are engaged in applying defensive or counter-attacking moves, and the eyes should express the intent behind these movements. The *Tai Chi Chuan Lun* (*Discourse*) states:

If, in certain places, the timing and
movements are not good,
The body will then move arbitrarily and
without co-ordination.
This fault will certainly be located in
the waist and the upper leg.
Above and below, forward and back,
left and right are all like this.
In general all this is controlled by the *Yi*
and not externally.

Indeed it is largely this emphasis on the
concept of *Yi* that has led to Tai Chi
Chuan being classified as a so-called
internal martial art.

Let us now return to the requirement
that there should be a smooth transition
from one technique to another. Many
writers refer to Tai Chi Chuan movements
as being circular, but this is only partly
true. The movements characteristically
involve spiral and focus, yet without any
halting at the point of focus – in contrast
to so-called external martial arts. But how
can we keep the movements smooth and
continuous, yet at the same time focus the
techniques properly? Again the answer is
given in the *Tai Chi Chuan Discourse*:

Fig 31   Stepping Back to Ride The Tiger
in Belgium.

You must clearly distinguish between
void and substantial;
Each place has of course its balance of
void and substantial,
Everywhere there is a union of void and
substantial.
The whole body is strung together
without the slightest discontinuity.
Long Boxing is like the *Chang Jiang*,
Surging and flowing without
interruption.

The smooth transition from one technique
to another is therefore accomplished by
shifting the body or stance and thus leading the limbs and/or by moving to almost
an extreme in one direction until we feel
that the hips and limbs are like coiled
springs; then we can use this feeling by

uncoiling in the opposite direction, as in
Snake Creeps Down.

The analogy of the Chang Jiang is an
interesting one. The Chang Jiang (literally
Long River) is the longest river in China;
it moves through vastly changing terrain
and is by turns slow and fast as it turns
and twists its way from Qinghai and Tibet
in the west to Shanghai in the east, 6,300
kilometres from its source. So like a river,
the form flows – but not at a uniform
speed. Generally it should be done slowly. If too slow, however, the movements
become stilted and do not flow; and if too
fast, they become jerky, the breathing
becomes more shallow and the circulatory benefits of the form decrease.

It is the character of the movements
which dictates the speed of the form, just
as the terrain through which a river is
passing dictates the speed of the river.
Thus more gymnastically difficult
movements such as Sweep Lotus Leg can

be done more briskly than less demanding techniques such as Grasping Bird's Tail.

Balanced Turning and Stepping

Let us now consider balanced turning and stepping, which to a large extent is the corollary of good posture and stance and correctly distinguishing Yin and Yang. First, many students have poor balance because they are top heavy, and this in turn is usually due to their failure to sink and to keep their centre of gravity low. Turning and stepping, as opposed to just turning, presents additional difficulties, particularly with foot placement. For example many students, after performing a kick, lower the kicking foot to the ground so that it is either off line leading to difficulties in performing the next technique, or they place the kicking foot too close or too far from the foot of the supporting leg.

One of the advantages of performing the form slowly (whether doing round form or square form) is that correction of faults becomes easier as there is more time to think. and thus transfers of weight are more gradual.

As regards turning, in my own style we perform turns differently depending on whether we are doing square form or round form. In square form, most turns are made on the heel, whereas in round form turns are usually made on the heel and then the toe. Supposedly, older people find it easier to learn in this way, before moving on to the round form method. I find this argument somewhat unconvincing, although the method does seem to work for older students.

With certain techniques we have a choice as to how to perform them, a fact that not everyone is aware of. For example in my own style, when performing the long form, two kicks with the left foot follow one another immediately: agile youths can manage to perform the first kick spin through 135 degrees and do the second one without replacing the foot on the ground; creaking veterans find it easier to replace the left foot on the ground before turning to make the second kick.

Complex techniques like this are a test, and unless there is a problem with health, most students eventually graduate to doing it the hard way.

Relaxation and Softness

We are often told that muscular strength must never be used when practising Tai Chi Chuan, that there should be no tension. Soft is good, hard is bad. Or is it? First of all, what is meant by 'relaxation' and 'softness'? Also, why is it desirable to be relaxed and soft, and how should we achieve this blissful state?

The Chinese terms for 'relaxation' and 'softness' which are used in Tai Chi Chuan are 'Song' for 'relaxed', and 'Rou', 'Mian' and 'Yuan' for 'softness'. The character 'Song', originally referring to hair, means 'loose', 'lax' and by extension 'relaxed'; Tai Chi masters often talk about being 'Qing Song', meaning light and relaxed.

When 'hard' and 'soft' are mentioned in a martial context, for example in Go-ju Ryu karate, the term for 'soft' is the Chinese character 'Rou'; when broken down to its components it means 'a slender stem', and by extension it means 'pliant', 'flexible' or 'elastic'. Mian literally means 'cotton', and this type of softness is referred to when discussing pushing hands. 'Yuan' meaning 'soft' or 'tender' is another term sometimes used to refer to Tai Chi Chuan.

Having defined some of the terms used, we can see that relaxation and softness are not such simple concepts. These terms do not mean that there is an absence of muscular movement or muscular tension, but that there is no stiffness, which is quite a different thing. Muscular strength is, and should be employed in practising the hand form, but this strength is trained, and it is relaxed and contains a high degree of elasticity. This concept of softness can also be explained with reference to the Tai Chi symbol in which there is a dot of Yin in the Yang, and vice versa – therefore there is no pure softness in the form. How soft should, or can you be?

Many Tai Chi Chuan practitioners have this softness to a higher degree than others, including myself. This does not mean that they are more skilful or knowledgeable, or even that their form looks any better; it is purely a difference in training regimen. Moreover, if you only practise the soft, or Yin aspects of Tai Chi Chuan, then you cannot be said to have the full art. Likewise if you only practise the hard, or Yang aspects, you have less than half the art because these two aspects complement one another to such a high degree. Those who want to possess the whole art will practise both aspects.

Softness is an admirable quality, but not in isolation. So why is it so important? If techniques are done slowly and softly, the body becomes more relaxed, and if we are relaxed we can move faster and more efficiently; this is one of the major reasons why so many hard-style karate and kung fu masters also train in Tai Chi Chuan. As the *Fighter's Song* has it: 'Appear relaxed, but don't be flaccid'.

How to achieve softness? Correct slow practice of the hand form techniques, the twelve Yin *Nei Kung* exercises and various ancillary exercises, some of which are to be found in pushing hands drills, all help to develop the required level of softness.

Finally, to perform Tai Chi Chuan form well, it is necessary that the techniques should be both aesthetically pleasing and contain martial spirit. It is not enough that the movements merely look pretty or gymnastically difficult and that the practitioner wears silk pyjamas; neither is it enough that the movements look strong, when in fact they are crude, and that absurd sounds such as Heng and Ha are emitted with hard use of force.

THE INNER FORM

Part of the inside-the-door training of Tai Chi Chuan is being shown the techniques of the inner form: this consists of a number of techniques which are not named or referred to in any way in ordinary classes – yet they do have names. However, their names and applications are normally only taught after *Bai Shi*, and as a result most Tai Chi practitioners are not only quite ignorant of these, but don't even know there is such a thing as an inner form. Because this knowledge is dying out, however, all the names of the inner form techniques are given here; I have not shown the applications.

THE SQUARE LONG FORM

At the time of writing this is the fullest long form to be found in any English language book on Tai Chi Chuan; the names of the techniques of the inner form are included in bold type in parentheses (as already indicated, these are not usually taught to students until after they have undergone *Bai Shi*).

As well as the many obvious and definite techniques of the inner form, other aspects of certain 'inside-the-door' techniques can also be said to exist in the flowing movements of the round long form. These include techniques such as Flying Flower Palm, Five Element Arm and Gyrating Arms. Round forms are best learned direct from a teacher, or if this is not possible, through video or CD ROM.

The form shown here is the square long form, in which the techniques are broken down and simplified so that it is easy for the student to follow the teacher and for the teacher to correct the student: it is used as a teaching tool before the student is taught the round long form. The square form is done to a count of 'One, two, three', most techniques being completed on the count of three; sometimes this means that to fit this format, the counting for an individual technique will vary, depending on where it occurs in the form. The square form is also useful in developing correct posture and focus. Moreover the individual techniques, including the techniques of the inner form, are more clear cut than when they appear in the round form, so their names and applications are easier to remember.

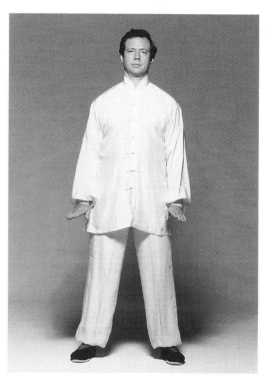

1.1

1. The Ready Style (*Wu Chi*: No Ultimate)

1. Place the feet a shoulder-width apart. Let the arms hang down at the sides with the wrists bent so that the palms face the ground. Relax and breathe naturally.
1a. Lower the palms so that the fingertips point down to the ground.

2. The Tai Chi Beginning Style

1. Raise the arms to shoulder level.
2. Draw the arms in by bending the elbows.
3. Lower the arms to the sides.
(Vanguard Arms)
4. Bend the knees.
5. Raise the left foot, heel first, then step forwards, resting the heel on the ground.

2.1

2.2

2.5

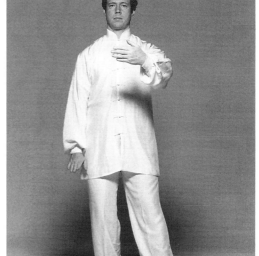

2.6

2.7

2.9

6. In a circular motion, bring the left hand round so that the palm faces the chest.
7. Bring the right hand round until it is between the left hand and the chest.
8. Turn the left foot in, resting the sole on the ground.
(Extend the Arms)
9. Lean forward by straightening the right leg and bending the left.

3. The Seven Stars Style

1. Reach out with the right hand at an angle of 45 degrees to the right.
2. Raise the right heel and, pivoting on the right toes, turn the body to the right.
3. Step forwards onto the right heel, bringing the right wrist and the left fingertips into contact.

4. Grasping The Bird's Tail

1. Bending at the waist, draw the arms in by bending the elbows out; the right palm faces up and the left palm faces down.
2. Shift forward, into a front stance, simultaneously stretching the arms out forwards and to the left. The right arm is almost straight.
3. Draw the arms across to the right by twisting the hips.
4. Lean back by bending the left leg and straightening the right.
5. Bending at the waist, press down with the right palm.
6. Shift forwards into a front stance, pushing out diagonally with the right hand.

5. The Single Whip

1. Keeping the right arm outstretched, bring the right hand round to the left in an

3.3

4.1

4.2

4.3

4.4

4.5

4.6

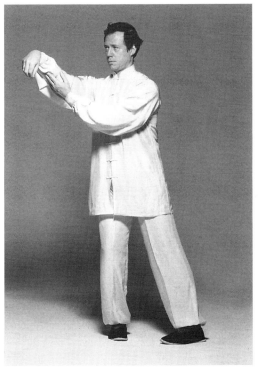

5.1

5.3

arc, at the end of which the hand forms a hook. At the same time the right foot turns in slightly towards the centre.

2. Take a small step to the left with the left foot.

3. Sweep the left hand across the body, palm facing inwards. As it passes the body, turn the left hand and push out, sitting down in a horse-riding stance.

6. Flying Oblique

1. Shift the weight onto the left foot, straightening the right leg and turning the right foot out so it points to the right. At the same time stretch out the hands as if flying.

6.1

7.1

7. Raise Hands And Step Up

(Single Seizing the Leg)

1. In a circular motion, bring the right hand round so that the palm faces the chest. At the same time bring the right foot 90 degrees across to the left, and place the heel on the ground.

(Double Seizing the Legs)

2. Bring the left hand round so it is between the right hand and the chest.

3. Lean forwards straightening the left leg and bending the right.

4. Step up with the left foot so the feet are parallel, keeping the knees bent and straightening the back.

5. Straightening the legs, raise the right hand and lower the left arm to the side.

7.3

7.4

7.5

8.1

8.2

8.   White Crane Flaps Its Wings

1. Bend at the waist.
2. Twist 90 degrees to the left.
(Break Arm Style)
3. Bring the left hand up in a circular motion so it is level with the right. The

fingertips should be a few inches apart.

4. Stand erect. The arms are arched above the head.

5. Turn to face the front.

6. Lower the hands to chest level, turning the right arm inwards so that the right palm faces the chest while the fingers point left.

8.3

8.4

8.5

9.2

8.6

9. Brush Knee Twist Step

1. Bending the knees, pivot 90 degrees to the left on the right toes and left heel. The weight is on the right leg; the hands point straight ahead.
2. Moving the left foot slightly left, draw the hands back just below the right ear.
3. Shift forwards into a front stance by straightening the right leg and bending the left. At the same time lower the left hand to the side, and push forwards with the right hand.

10. The Seven Stars Style (Left

1. Shift the weight back onto the right foot.

9.3

2. Draw the right arm in by sinking the elbow.

3. Raise the left hand and touch the wrist against the right fingertips.

11. Brush Knee Twist Step

1. Raise the right hand so the fingers point to the left hand.

2. Twisting at the waist, draw the hands back to just below the right ear.

3. Shift forwards into a front stance by straightening the right leg and bending the left. At the same time lower the left hand to the side and push forward with the right hand. (Repeat 9. 3.)

4. Step forwards with the right leg, placing the heel on the ground.

5. Twisting at the waist, draw the hands back to just below the left ear. (Mirror image 9. 2.)

6. Shift forwards into a front stance, lowering the right hand to the side and pushing forwards with the left hand. (Mirror image 9. 3.)

7. Step forwards with the left leg, resting the heel on the ground.

8. Repeat 9. 2.

9. Repeat 9. 3.

12. The Seven Stars Style (Left)

Repeat 10.

13. Stroke the Luke

1. Twisting the waist, turn the upper body to the right.

2. Lean forward, into a front stance, pushing the left arm out.

3. Twisting the waist, turn the upper body to the left.

13.3

13.4

14.2

13.6

4. Bring the right foot up so it is level with the left; the weight rests evenly on both legs.
5. Draw the hands in by bending the elbows out to the side.
6. Stand up straight.

14. Step Up, Parry and Punch

1. Bend the knees and step forwards, resting the left heel on the ground.
2. Draw the hands back to the right hip, forming a fist with the right hand, then shift forwards into a front stance, bringing the hands forwards in an arc.
3. Shifting the weight back onto the right leg, draw the right fist back to the hip, knuckles facing out to the right.

14.3

14.4

14.5

14.6

4. Twisting the body to the right, sweep the left hand across to the right.

5. Turning the left arm so the left palm faces the ground, turn the body to the left and draw the left arm across.

6. Shifting forwards into a front stance, give a straight punch with the right hand and rest the left palm on the right forearm.

15. As If Shutting a Door

1. Place the left palm against the underside of the right wrist.

2. Lean back, bringing the arms back; both palms face the body.

3. Shifting into a front stance, push forwards.

15.2

16. Embrace the Tiger and Return to Mountain

1. Turning the left foot on its heel 90 degrees to the right, draw the hands down to the left thigh.

2. Pivoting on the right heel, turn to the right and rest the backs of the hands on the thighs.

3. Shift the weight onto the right leg, stretching the arms diagonally out to the side.

15.3

16.3

17.1

same time, pivot on the left heel 90 degrees to the right.

2. Turn the body round to the right by pivoting on the right heel. Keeping the hands just below the left ear, move the right heel a little out to the right.

3. Shift forwards into a front stance, lowering the right hand to the side and pushing forwards with the left hand. At the same time, turn the left foot on the heel so it points forwards.

20.   The Seven Stars Style (Right)

Mirror image of 10.

21.   Grasping Bird's Tail

Repeat 4.

22.   Oblique Single Whip

Repeat 5.

17.   Cross Hands

1. Bring the left foot up level with the right, at the same time crossing the hands in front of the chest. Now stand up straight.

18.   Oblique Brush Knee Twist Step

1. Bending the knees, step out at 45 degrees, resting the left heel on the ground. Repeat 9. 2.

2. Repeat 9. 3.

19.   Turn Body, Brush Knee Twist Step

1. Raise the left hand so it is in front of, and palm facing the right palm. At the

23.1

23. Fist Under Elbow

1. Turn to face the left by pivoting on the left heel through 45 degrees. At the same time reach round and out to the left with the left hand.

2. Sweep the right hand round in an arc until the inside of the hand touches the left palm, simultaneously shifting into a front stance by stepping slightly to the right with the right foot.

3. Lean the weight back on the right leg, forming both hands into fists as they are drawn in towards the body. The right fist is under the left elbow.

23.3

23.2

24. Step Back and Repulse Monkey

1. Twist the waist to the right and then, shifting into a front stance, twist back to the left, stretching out the left arm, palm open and facing up. The right fist remains clenched.

2. Shift the weight back onto the right leg and twisting at the waist, draw back both hands palms open to just below the left ear.

3. Step back with the left foot into a front stance, pushing forwards with the left hand and lowering the right hand to the right side.

4. Shift the weight back onto the left leg.

5. Twisting the waist, draw the hands back to just below the right ear. (The final stance is a mirror image of 24. 2.)

24.1

24.3

24.2

6. Step back with the right foot into a front stance, pushing forwards with the right hand and lowering the left hand to the left side. (Mirror image of 24. 3.)
7. Shift the weight back.
8. Repeat 24. 2.
9. Repeat 24. 3.

25. Flying Oblique (Low)

1. Turn the left arm so the palm faces up.
2. Place the right fingertips on the left wrist.
3. Pivoting on the right heel, turn the right foot to the right and squat down.
(High)
4. Step forwards with the left leg so it is outstretched with the heel on the ground.
5. Place the sole of the left foot on the ground so it is parallel with the right.
6. Pivoting on the right foot and shifting the weight onto the left leg, turn to face

25.3

the right and stretch out the hands as if flying.

26.   Raise Hands and Step Up

1. to 6. Repeat 7.1. to 7.5.

27.   White Crane Flaps Its Wings

Repeat 8.

28.   Brush Knee Twist Step

Repeat 9.

29.   The Seven Stars Style (Left)

Repeat 10.

30.   Needle at Sea Bottom

1. Draw back the left foot, placing the toes in contact with the ground.
2. Bring the right hand up above the left so it points diagonally downwards.

25.5

30.3

3. Sink down, thrusting the right hand towards the ground and drawing the left hand back towards the right shoulder.

31. Fan Through the Back

1. Step forwards placing the left heel on the ground.
2. Shift forwards into a front stance, bringing the right arm up to shoulder height.
3. Turn the left foot 90 degrees in to the right, turning the right arm anticlockwise through 180 degrees and simultaneously sliding the left palm along the right arm.
4. Step back with the right foot, diagonally and to the right.

31.6

31.5

5. Sit down in a horse-riding stance, drawing the hands in slightly.
6. Push out with the left hand, drawing the right hand up above the head. The movement resembles opening a fan.

32. Turn Body and Swing Fist

1. Turn on the heels to face the right, bringing the left hand, fist clenched, down to the left side.
2. Forming a fist with the right hand, lower it to the left side behind the left fist.
3. Shifting into a front stance, open the left hand and swing both hands forwards in an arc so the left palm is above the clenched right fist.

32.1

32.2

32.3

33. Step Back, Parry and Punch

1. Shift the weight back onto the left leg.
2. Stepping back with the right foot into a front stance, draw the arms down and then round in a full circle.
3.–6. Repeat 14.3.–6.

34. Step Up, Grasping Bird's Tail

(Reverse Seven Stars)

1. Shift the weight back onto the right leg, opening the right hand and bringing the left fingertips up to the right wrist.
2. Bend at the waist, drawing the arms in slightly. Right palm faces up.
3. Shift into a front stance, pushing the arms forwards.

36.1

36.2

36.3

36.4

36.6

4. Step forwards with the right foot resting the heel on the ground.

5.–9. Repeat 4. 2.–6.

35. The Single Whip

Repeat 5.

36. Wave Hands in Clouds (also known as Turning Hands)

1. Turn the right foot out at 45 degrees to the right by pivoting on the right heel, at the same time shifting the weight onto the right leg and reaching out at 45 degrees to the right with the right hand.

2. Lowering the left hand, bring it across and then up in a semicircle until the fingertips touch the underside of the right wrist. At the same time move into a full front stance by turning the left foot in on the heel.

3. Sweep the left hand round and up to the left, simultaneously turning the left foot 90 degrees to the left and shifting the weight onto the left foot.

4. Turn the body into a front stance facing diagonally out to the left, at the same time turning the left hand, palm down, and lowering the right hand to the thigh.

5. Step up with the right foot touching the right heel against the left so that the feet form a 'V'.

6. Raise the right hand until the fingertips touch the left wrist, at the same time sinking down slightly and keeping the back straight.

7. Draw the right hand across and up to the right, pivoting on the right heel in the same direction, but continuing to look left.

8. In one movement, turn to face diagonally out to the right by pivoting on the ball of the left foot, lower the left hand to the thigh and turn the right hand so the palm faces to the ground.

9. Step back to the left with the left foot to form a front stance, at the same time raising the left hand till the fingertips touch the right wrist.

10. Sweep the left hand round and up to the left, simultaneously turning the left foot 90 degrees to the left and shifting the weight onto the left foot.

11. Move into a front stance facing diagonally out to the left, at the same time turning the left hand palm down and lowering the right hand to the thigh.

12. Step up with the right foot, bringing the heels together to form a 'V', at the same time bringing the right fingertips up

38.1

38.3

to touch the left wrist. Sink down lightly and keep the back straight during the movement.
13.–15. Repeat 36. 7.–9.

37. The Single Whip

Repeat 5.

38. Pat the Horse High (Left)

1. Pivoting on the heels to the left, shift the weight back onto the right leg and raise the open right hand to head level. The left palm is face up.

2. Draw the left foot back and rest the toes on the ground.
3. Bring the right wrist and left fingertips into contact by lowering the right arm and drawing in the left. Sink down in the stance at the same time.
4. Step out with the left leg, placing the heel on the ground.

39. Left Drape Body

1. Shift into a front stance, turning the elbows out until the right palm is directly above and facing the left palm.
(Separate Hands)

39.1

39.2

2. Twist the waist to the right and then back to the left, stretching the left arm out, palm up, at 45 degrees to the left, while the gaze follows the right hand which reaches out to the right at 45 degrees, palm down.

(Tiger Embraces Head)

3. Turn 45 degrees to the left on the left heel, bringing the right wrist across to touch the left, lightly clenching the fists.

4. Sweep the right foot across in front of the left, resting the ball of the foot on the ground.

5. Straighten the back by sinking down in the stance.

39.3

39.5

40.1

40.3

40. Right Separate Legs

1. Raise the right leg. The left leg is slightly bent.
2. Open the hands, turning them palm down and drawing them apart slightly.
3. Turning the body to the right, kick out in a curve with the right leg at 45 degrees, pointing the toes out. The right arm follows the right leg out to the right, while the left hand reaches back and to the left.

41. Pat Horse High (Right)

1. Place the right heel on the ground. The left hand is at head level, while the right hand is palm up, fingers pointing forwards.

42. Right Drape Body

Mirror image of 39.

43. Left Separate Leg

Mirror image of 40.

44. Turn Round and Kick with Heel

1. Draw the left leg back behind the right, resting the toes on the ground. At the same time, lightly clenching the fists, bring the arms in until the left wrist covers the right.
2. Pivoting on the right heel, bring the body round through 180 degrees anti-clockwise to face the opposite direction.
3. Raise the left leg and kick forwards with the heel at waist level. The left arm follows the left leg, while the right arm reaches back and to the right. The palms are open.

44.1

44.3

46.3

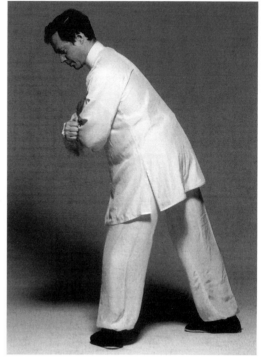

47.1

45.   Brush Knee Twist Step

1. Place the left heel on the ground.
2.–6. Repeat 11. 2.–6.

46.   Step Forwards and Plant Punch

1. Step forwards with the left leg, placing the heel on the ground.
2. Twisting at the waist, draw the hands back to just below the right ear.
3. Shift forwards into a front stance, drawing a circle in the air with the left hand by bringing it down and out to the left. As the left hand moves back in towards the body, punch straight down with the right fist. Complete the circle by resting the left hand on the right forearm as the right fist completes the punch.

47.   Turn Body and Swing Fist

1. Turn the left foot 90 degrees in towards the centre, at the same time folding the right arm over the left.
2. Pivoting on the right heel, turn the body clockwise through 180 degrees to face the opposite direction. Step slightly to the right on the right heel.
3. Leaning forwards into a front stance, swing the arms forwards in an arc, bringing the left palm into position above the clenched right fist.

47.3

51.1

48. Step Up and Pat Horse High (Left)

1. Step forwards, placing the left heel on the ground. At the same time unclenching the right fist, turn the hands anticlockwise through 180 degrees so that the right palm is above the left, and the left fingertips touch the right wrist.

49. Left Drape Body

50. Right Separate Legs

51. Step Back Seven Stars Style

1. Step diagonally back with the right foot, keeping the weight forwards. The hands remain in position.

2. Shift the weight back onto the right leg, simultaneously bending the right arm by sinking the elbow.

3. Draw the left arm in until the wrist comes into contact with the right fingertips. At the same time, turn the left foot on the heel so that the toes are raised and point forwards.

51.3

52.1

52. Step Back to Strike the Tiger

1. Step back with the left leg into a front stance, at the same time turning the palms face down and extending the right arm out over the left.

2. Pivoting on the left heel 90 degrees to the left, shift the weight onto the left leg and straighten the right leg, lowering the hands to just above the right thigh.

3. Shift into a front stance by turning the right foot 180 degrees around to the left, simultaneously bring the left hand up to protect the forehead and the right hand round to protect the groin.

52.3

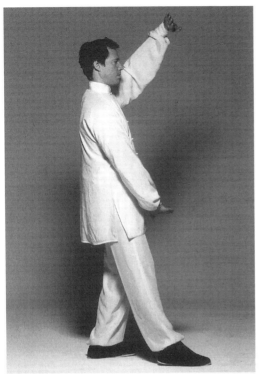

53.1

53.2

53. Twist the Body and Kick

1. Turn the left foot in towards the centre. Sliding in on the ball of the right foot, draw it in towards the left foot, simultaneously twisting the body 135 degrees round to the right.
2. Twisting the waist to the left, raise the right arm in a 180 degrees arc. At the top of the arc the left arm follows the right arm down and across to the right in another 180 degrees arc. At the bottom of this arc, clench the fists as the right hand comes to rest, palm facing the navel, to complete a circle. The left hand continues round to complete a circle, coming to rest above the head, while the right leg is raised with the sole of the foot turned up and facing left.
3. Stretching the arms out to the side at shoulder level, palms down, kick out to the right at knee level with the outside of the right foot.

109

53.3

54.3

54. Box the Ears

1. Place the right heel on the ground and draw the arms in so they are parallel in front of the chest.
2. Lean forwards into a front stance, lowering the hands to thigh level.
3. Clench the fists and bring them up in an arc as if to strike the ears of an opponent.

55. Right Drape Body

Mirror image of 39. 3.–5.

56. Left Separate Legs

Repeat 43.

57. Turn Round and Kick with the Heel

1. Lower the left leg, crossing it over the right. simultaneously clenching the fists and bringing the wrists into contact in front of the body.
2. Pivot 180 degrees around to the right on the left heel and right toes.
3. Raise the right leg and kick forwards with the heel. The right arm follows the

57.1

right leg, while the left arm reaches back and to the left. The palms are open.

58. Swing the Fist

1. Place the right heel on the ground.
2. Clench the fists and lower the arms to the left side, left over right. (Repeat 32. 2.)
3. Shifting into a front stance, open the left hand and swing both hands forward in an arc so the left palm is above the clenched right fist. (Repeat 32. 3.)

59. Step Up, Parry and Punch

Repeat 14.

60. As If Shutting the Door

Repeat 15.

61. Embrace Tiger and Return to Mountain

Repeat 16.

62. Cross Hands

Repeat 17.

63. Turn Body, Brush Knee Twist Step

Repeat 18.

64. Oblique Brush Knee Twist Step

Repeat 19.

65. The Seven Stars Style

Repeat 20. (Mirror image of 10.)

66. Grasping Bird's Tail

Repeat 4.

67. Oblique Single Whip

Repeat 5.

68. The Seven Stars Style

1. Turn the left foot in towards the centre.
2. Bring the left hand into the body and bring the right foot in.
3. Bring the right wrist onto the left fingertips. (Mirror image of 10. 3.)

69. Parting the Wild Horse's Mane

1. Twist the hips to the left and lower the

111

69.1

right hand to just below the left hip, palm up.

2. Step slightly to the right with the right leg and shift into a front stance, twisting the hips to the left.

3. Stretch out the arms by reaching out at 45 degrees to the right with the right arm palm up, while the gaze follows the left hand which reaches out to the left at 45 degrees .

70.   The Seven Stars Style

1. Shift the weight back onto the left leg.
2.–3. Repeat 68. 2.–3.

71.   Parting the Wild Horse's Mane

1.–3. Repeat 69. 1.–3.
4. Turn the right foot on the heel 90 degrees out to the right and draw the right

69.3

71.4

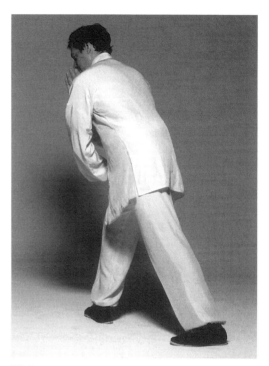

71.5

73. Parting the Wild Horse's Mane

Repeat 71. 1.–6.

74. Fair Lady Works at Shuttle

1. Shift forward into a front stance, swinging the left arm out to the left with the right fingertips resting on the left arm joint.
2. Shift the weight back onto the right leg, drawing the left arm in by sinking the elbow. Twist at the waist to the right.
3. Shift forwards into a front stance and push out to the left with both hands. The face is framed by the left arm which is above the head and the right arm which is in front of the body.

hand in until the back of the thumb faces the left breast.
5. Twisting the hips to the right, lower the left-hand palm to below the right hip.
6. Step forwards onto the left heel.
7. Shift forwards into a front stance.
8. Twist the hips to the right.
9. Stretch out the arms by reaching out at 45 degrees to the left with the left-hand palm up while the gaze follows the right hand which reaches out to the right at 45 degrees . At the same time twist the hips to the left.
10.–15. Mirror image of 71. 4.–9.

72. The Seven Stars Style

Repeat 70.

74.1

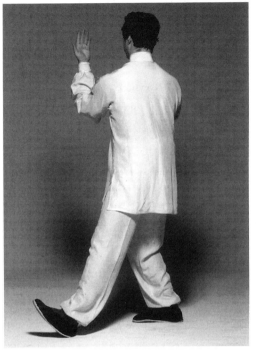

74.2

74.3

4. Pivot on the left heel to the right and draw the arms in so the right arm is at waist level, palm up, while the left is palm down above the right.

5. Turn 180 degrees around to the right by pivoting on the right heel and then stepping slightly out to the right with the right heel.

6. Shift forwards into a front stance, swinging the right arm round to the right with the left fingertips resting on the right arm joint.

7. Shift the weight back onto the left leg and draw the right arm in by sinking the elbow.

8. Twist at the waist to the left.

9. Shift forwards into a front stance and push out to the right with both hands. The face is framed by the right arm which is curved above the head and the left hand which is in front of the body.

75. The Seven Stars Style

Repeat 70.

76. Parting the Horse's Mane

Repeat 71. 1.–6.

77. Fair Lady Works at Shuttle

Mirror image of 74. 1.–9

78. The Seven Stars Style

Repeat 70.

79. Grasping the Bird's Tail

Repeat 4.

80. Single Whip

Repeat 5.

81. Cloud Hands (also known as Turning Hands)

Repeat 36.

82. The Single Whip

Repeat 5.

83. Snake Creeps Down

1. Pivoting on the left heel, shift the weight onto the left leg and reach out to the left with the left hand.
2. Twisting the hips, reach over and across to the left with the right hand until the wrist touches the left fingertips. At the same time, turn the right foot in towards the centre.

83.1

83.2

3. Turning the right foot on its heel so it points diagonally out to the right, reach over and across past the right hand with the left hand. The left forearm rests against the right fingertips.

4. Shift the weight back onto the right leg, straightening the left leg and pulling the hands in close to the body. The left foot is flat on the ground.

5. Draw the hands in an arc to the right and then down just above the ground in front of the body, sinking down at the same time.

6. Shift forwards and up into a front stance, stepping out slightly with the right foot, bringing the left hand up in an arc to protect the face, while the right hand protects the groin.

83.3

83.5

83.6

84.2

84.1

84. Golden Cockerel Stands on One Leg Right

1. Raise the right leg, turning the sole to face left. At the same time raise the right hand above the forehead and lower the left hand.

(White Snake Spits out its Tongue)

2. Lower the right heel, bring both hands palm up in towards the centre; the left fingertips touch the centre of the right forearm.

3. Shift into a front stance, pushing the left arm forwards over the right so the right fingertips rest against the centre of the left forearm.

4. Kick out at knee level with the toes of the left foot.

117

84.4

85.1

85. Step Back and Repulse Monkey

(Golden Cockerel on One Leg Left)
1. Twist the hips to the left, drawing the hands back to ear level, simultaneously drawing back the left leg by bending the knee.
2.–8. Repeat 24. 2.–9.

86. Step Aside, Flying Oblique

1.–4. Repeat 25. 1.–4.
5. Step back with the left leg, placing the sole on the ground.
6. Shift the weight back onto the left leg and stretch out the hands as if flying.

87. Raise Hands and Step Up

(Double Seizing Legs)
1. Turning the left foot in towards the centre, press forwards with the hands in front of the body, palms facing, and lean forwards into a front stance. (Final position as in 7. 3.)
2.–3. Repeat 7. 4.–5.

88. White Crane Flaps Its Wings

Repeat 8.

89. Brush Knee Twist Step

Repeat 9.

90. The Seven Stars Style

Repeat 10.

91. Needle at Sea Bottom

Repeat 30.

92. Fan Through the Back

Repeat 31.

93. Turn Body Swing Fist

Repeat 32.

94. Step Up, Parry and Punch

1. Step forwards resting the left heel on the ground. (Final position as in 14. 1.)
2.–6. Repeat 14. 2.–6.

95. Step Up, Grasping Bird's Tail

Repeat 34.

96. The Single Whip

Repeat 5.

97. Cloud Hands (also known as Turning Hands)

Repeat 36.

98. The Single Whip

Repeat 5.

99. Pat Horse High (Left)

Repeat 38.

100. Slap the Face

1. Step out with the left leg and rest the heel on the ground.
2. Twisting the hips to the left, swing the left hand up and out to the left, palm up. The right hand is drawn in to protect the left armpit, palm down.
3. Shifting forwards into a front stance, the left hand slaps forwards and down into the opponent's face.

100.2

119

100.3

101.1

101.   Cross and Single Hand Sweep Lotus Leg

1. Pivot 180 degrees around to the right on the heels, sweeping the left hand across the body to the right. The right hand is under the left armpit and the weight is on the left leg.
2. Raise the right leg.
3. Slap the right toes with the left hand by sweeping the hand to the left and the right leg to the right.

102.   Brush Knee Twist Step

1. Lower the right heel to the ground.
2.–3. Mirror image of 9. 2.–3.

101.3

103. Step Up to Punch the Groin

1. Step forwards with the left leg, resting the heel on the ground.
2. Twisting at the waist, draw the hands back to just below the right ear.
3. Shift forwards into a front stance, bringing the left hand down and out to the left. Continue the movement of the left hand so that it comes up and in again towards the body, at the same time clenching the right fist, bringing it round and up in an arc. The left hand completes the circle it has drawn by resting on the right forearm as the right fist completes the punch.

104. Step Up, Grasping the Bird's Tail

Repeat 34.

105. The Single Whip

Repeat 5.

106. Snake Creeps Down

Repeat 83.

107. Step Up, Seven Stars

1. Cross the hands in front of the body, left over right, and at the same time step forwards with the right foot, resting the ball of the foot on the ground and keeping the weight on the left leg. Lean back slightly as you step forwards.

108. Step Back to Ride the Tiger

1. Step back with the right leg into a front

103.3

107.1

108.3

108.6

108.4

stance. Lean forwards slightly.

2. Shift the weight back onto the rear leg, the ball of the foot comes up.

3. Draw the left leg back, touching the ground with the toes.

4. Bring both hands down and out to the side in an arc. The left hand forms a hook, wrist bent, while the right palm is open and facing right.

5. Pivoting on the left toes, twist the hips to the right. The left arm moves round and down in an arc until the fingertips are pointing away from the body. At the same time the right hand comes up to protect the head.

6. Kick straight forward with the left leg at groin level.

109. Turn Body and Slap the Face

1. Pivoting 90 degrees around to the right on the right foot, swing the left hand up and out to the left, palm up. The right hand is drawn in to protect the left armpit.

2. Step down into a front stance, slapping forwards into the opponent's face while the right hand protects the armpit. (Final position as in 100. 3.)

110. Turn Body and Double Hand Sweep Lotus Leg

1. Pivoting on the heels, turn 180 degrees around to the right and sweep the hands across the body to the right.

110.1

110.2

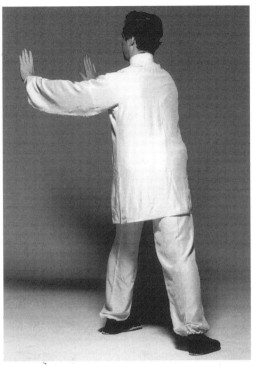

111.1

110.3

2. Swing the right leg out to the left. Slap the toes with both hands by sweeping the hands to the left as the right leg swings back across to the right.

3. Place the right foot on the ground behind the left, sweeping the hands to the left and keeping the weight on the left leg.

111. Draw the Bow to Shoot the Tiger

1. Turning to the right, shift the weight onto the right leg and lower the hands just below waist level.

2. Twisting the waist to the right, swing the arms round to the right hip, palm down. The gaze is directed back over the right shoulder.

3. Raise the hands to shoulder level so the right arm is straight while the left arm

111.3

111.6

is bent as if drawing a bow.
4. Clench the fists.
5. Turn to face the front, drawing the fists in towards the body.
6. Punch forwards with both fists, palms facing out to the right.

112. Pat the Horse High (Left)

1. Step forwards with the left foot, resting the heel on the ground. Open the hands, lowering the right palm and drawing in the left until the right wrist touches the left fingertips.

113. Slap the Face

Repeat 100. 2.–3.

114. Turn Body and Swing Fist

Repeat 47.

115. Step Up to Pat the Horse High

1. Step forwards with the left foot, resting the heel on the ground. At the same time unclench the right fist, turning the hand anticlockwise through 180 degrees so that the right palm is above the left and the left fingertips touch the right wrist. (Final position as in 112. 1.)

116. Step Up, Grasping the Bird's Tail

1. Move the hands round and down in an arc, clockwise through 180 degrees so that the left palm faces down and the right palm faces up. Then step forwards with the right foot into a front stance and stretch the arms diagonally out to the front. (Final position as in 4. 2.)
2.–5. Repeat 4. 3.–6.

117. The Single Whip

Repeat 5.

118. Tai Chi at Rest

1. Turn the right foot out at 45 degrees to the right by pivoting on the heel. At the same time, shift the weight onto the right leg and reach out at 45 degrees to the right with the right hand.

118.1

2. Bring the left foot across towards the right, turn the right foot in so the feet are parallel and the weight is evenly distributed, at the same time crossing the hands in front of the chest, left hand on the inside. Both knees are bent.

119. Completion Style

1. Lower the hands to the sides and straighten the legs to resume the first position (*Wu Chi*).

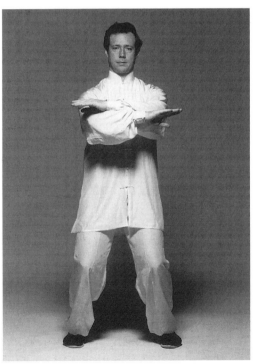

118.2

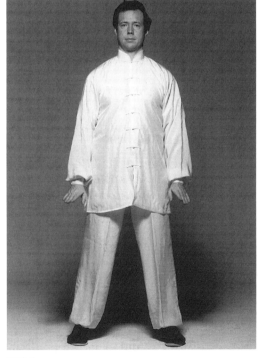

119.1

6 Strategies and Tactics

The Tai Chi Chuan fighting strategies are drawn from Taoistic ideas of Yin and Yang as applied to warfare by military strategists such as Sun Tzu; the tactics come from using the principles of Taoism to analyse and explain Tai Chi Chuan techniques. Those elucidated below can be used in different combinations, and may also be combined with other principles not listed here. They can be extended to all martial aspects of Tai Chi Chuan including the use of weapons.

THE MARTIAL ASPECT OF TAI CHI CHUAN

Stillness Defeats Motion

The first principle of Tai Chi Chuan in fighting is to use stillness to defeat motion. This is expressed in the saying:

> If the opponent doesn't move, I don't move.
> If the opponent starts to move, I move first.

Thus *Yin* is being used in the form of passivity, against *Yang* in the form of motion, and this has both defensive and attacking connotations. To do this requires coolness, a clear mind and expert timing. The opponent is allowed to commit himself to the attack, so that it is difficult for him to change what he is doing and he is vulnerable to counter-attack.

Softness Overcomes Hardness

> The Fighter's Song says:
> Allowing the opponent to attack me with great force,
> I use four taels [ounces] to displace one thousand catties [pounds].

The Tai Chi Chuan classics give various explanations of this method. In order to meet this requirement the defender needs to divert and/or evade attacks, rather than block them with great force: this is Yin. To a large extent this evasion and to some extent this diversion are trained in the pushing hands drills. After the diversion and/or evasion he counter-attacks immediately by striking, throwing or locking: this is Yang.

> The *Fighter's Song* goes on to say,
> 'Entice the opponent forward into the void, then promptly discharge'.

To create the void it is necessary either to divert the opponent's attack into emptiness, or to present him with emptiness by removing the target. To discharge involves striking or throwing the opponent. Similarly, 'If you can be light and agile you understand *Jin* [educated force]': in

Fig 32 Enticing the opponent into the void.

Fig 33 Promptly discharging.

other words it isn't enough just to learn techniques; it is also necessary to learn how to move efficiently.

The *Tai Chi Chuan Classic* (*Ching*) also gives useful advice on the subject of *San Shou*:

> When you feel pressure on the left, make the left empty.
> When you feel pressure on the right, make the right distant.
> A feather cannot be added, a fly cannot land. Others do not know me, I alone know them.

Fig 34 Making the left empty.

These extracts emphasize the importance of alertness and what is called 'listening ability' which is trained in pushing hands. They also demonstrate that Tai Chi Chuan practitioners should go with, rather than against an opponent's force, and should counter the opponent as soon as he has committed himself to a course of action.

FIVE CLOSE-QUARTER STRATEGIES

In Tai Chi Chuan there are five close-quarter strategies which are interrelated:

Nian

Nian can be written in two ways, and many Tai Chi books take the traditional and the simplified forms for this character as being in fact different characters. However, a perusal of any Chinese dictionary will reveal that they are one and the same. The character means 'sticking' or 'adherence', so at close quarters the arms should be as if glued to the opponent's, so that we can control him and strike, lock or throw him. While applying such techniques which can embrace vital point attacks, we are also preventing the opponent from doing anything to us.

Lian

Lian represents chariots moving in line, and by extension means 'continuous' or 'connected'. So at close quarters our defensive and countering movements should be continuous and connected.

Mian

Mian literally means 'cotton' and therefore has the idea of softness. It is often over-emphasized at the expense of other strategies and tactics: it is not that softness is good, but that softness at the right time and place is good; those who are soft have better listening abilities, can react faster, and when they suddenly *Hua* (divert) an attack and *Fa* (discharge), it is difficult for the opponent to react in time. Also they are better able to change from hard to soft and vice versa as appropriate.

Sui

Sui means 'to follow' or 'allow'. It is often translated as 'yielding', but I feel that this is misleading as it has mainly negative connotations, whereas *Sui* has the idea of moving forward, back, left or right in response to the opponent's actions. Again this skill is trained in pushing hands, particularly in moving step.

Bu Diu Ding

Bu means 'not', *Diu* means 'to lose'/'abandon', while *Ding* means 'to oppose'. In other words, we should neither lose contact with the opponent thus allowing him to launch a fresh assault, nor should we oppose his force with brute force thus wasting energy.

All of these strategies are trained in both moving and fixed-step pushing hands so that they become second nature. The idea behind them is to keep control of the opponent and to manoeuvre him off balance or into a disadvantageous position so that he can be struck, thrown, locked or choked.

THE THIRTEEN TACTICS (*SHI SAN SHI*)

The Thirteen Tactics are the Eight Forces (*Ba Jin*) combined with the Five Steps (*Wu Bu*). These tactics will be examined in turn.

Jin

Jin or *Jing* is one of the key concepts in Tai Chi Chuan. In the composition of the character, the radical is that part of it

Fig 35   Jin/Jing.

Fig. 37   Ching/Jing.

Fig 36   Li.

which gives a clue as to its meaning. For instance, the radical of *Jin* is *Li* which means 'strength', and it is usually explained as a drawing of a plough: it requires strength to use a plough, hence the meaning. An alternative explanation is that it evolved from the drawing of a sinew. The other part of the character gives it the sound.

Many readers will have heard of The Book of Changes, the *I Ching*/*Yi* Jing. In the character for *Ching*/*Jing*, the radical on the left means 'silk', as books at that time were written on silk. The other component is the same as for *Jin*. From this combination of the concepts of strength and education we can see how *Jin* in Tai Chi Chuan terminology has come to mean 'force' or 'power'. In Tai Chi Chuan parlance it is force with technique, in other words, trained force as opposed to brute force. It is often misleadingly translated as 'energy' by people who either wish to make Tai Chi Chuan more mysterious than it really is, or who wish to hide the martial aspects.

It is a great fallacy that Tai Chi Chuan practitioners should not use strength or force: it is the use of *brute* force and stiffness which is to be abjured. *Jin* is a type of *Li*, but *Li* is not always *Jin*, whereas brute force and stiffness are always *Li* and never *Jin*.

Jin can be Yin or Yang, hard or soft; defensive or offensive. It can be short distance or long distance; high or low. The ultimate aim in martial Tai Chi Chuan is to reach the stage of understanding *Jin*. It should also be elastic. This allows us to change between hard and soft or vice versa when defending or striking.

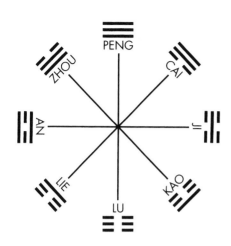

Fig 38   Eight Jin and Eight Trigrams.

Fig 39   Peng.

EIGHT JIN AND EIGHT TRIGRAMS

The Tai Chi classics mention *Ba Jin*, or Eight Forces, each of which is identified with a different trigram of the *Ba Gua* or Eight Trigrams based on the direction in which it is perceived that type of Jin is normally applied. Just as the interplay between the elements could be positive or negative and constantly changed, so we change our position to match the opponent. And just as the Eight Trigrams combine with one another to form the hexagrams of the *I Ching*, so the Eight Forces can be combined to form different techniques. Putting all this together gives a wide range of possible combinations.

I don't believe that someone using the Eight Trigrams invented eight types of *Jin* and from these produced all the techniques in Tai Chi Chuan. Apart from anything else, many of the techniques we use in Tai Chi Chuan do not conveniently fit into these eight types of *Jin*. It is almost certain that Eight Trigram theory was used to analyse and classify already existing techniques. However, these eight types of *Jin* can be trained in different ways, and are a useful means to analyse the various aspects of Tai Chi Chuan.

Because these techniques can be used in more than one way, I don't propose to use the common English translations for them, which are often very limited and misleading.

PENG (Fig 39): an upward-directed and usually circular force. If the opponent thrusts at your chest and you raise your hands to deflect his hands upwards, but also forwards causing him to lose balance, this is *Peng*. This makes his ribs vulnerable to a counter.

LU (Fig 40): a diversion to the side. If the opponent punches and you intercept with the arm and divert the attack slightly off course and into emptiness, this is *Lu*. In employing *Lu* to divert, our hand will generally intercept the opponent's arm at the wrist and/or elbow joints. The greater the force which he employs, the greater

131

Fig 40   Lu.

Fig 42   An.

Fig 43   Cai.

Fig 41   Ji.

his loss of balance, making him vulnerable to a counter.

JI (Fig 41): a forward-directed palm strike or push, after the opponent's attack has been avoided or redirected.

AN (Fig 42): a downward-directed force, such as pressing down on and at an angle to the opponent as he loses balance in a forward direction after a *Lu* diversion.

CAI (Fig 43): literally means 'to pluck', and in this context is usually translated as 'uprooting', it describes where in response to an opponent's attack we sink,

Fig 44   Lie.

Fig 46   Kao.

Fig 45   Zhou.

at the same time using leverage to disrupt his balance. The throwing application in Raise Hands Step Up is an example of this.

LIE (Fig 44): where spiralling force is used, for example where we initially divert the opponent's attack using *Lu*, then spiral his attacking arm back in towards him.

ZHOU (Fig 45): the use of the forearm or elbow either to divert an attack or to strike the face or ribs as we move forwards in response to a pull.

KAO (Fig 46): the use of the shoulder or body to strike the opponent in a similar way to *Zhou*.

These Eight *Jin* can be used either singly or in combination, providing a circle of defence and counter-attack. Often self-defence techniques contain elements of more than one *Jin*. Peng and Lu contain elements of one another, and *Lu* also contains some *Ji*. Lie contains *Cai* and *An*. Some authors talk of other types of *Jin* such as 'Reeling Silk *Jin*', but these really come under one or other of these eight classifications; 'Reeling Silk' is in fact primarily the use of *Lie* or spiralling *Jin*.

I don't usually teach beginners about these Eight Powers; they often find the forms, pushing hands and self defence difficult enough. However, instructors and more senior students should know about, and be able to explain these concepts, and they are a useful method of analysing techniques.

There are many techniques in Tai Chi Chuan which do not fit easily into any of these eight categories, for instance those employing foot and knee. In addition some contain elements of the others, so *Lie* has elements of *Peng*, *Lu* and *An*; but they are a useful way to analyse the form.

BU

Bu means 'steps' or 'footwork' or 'stance'. This term encompasses stances that we use, evasion, moving in and out of range, and shifting from one stance to another. The *Wu Bu* or Five Steps, which with the *Ba Jin* or Eight Forces form the Thirteen Tactics, are Advance Step, Retreat Step, Left Glance, Right Gaze, and Centrally Fixed. A wide variety of stances can be

used in these Five Steps. The stances are trained in the forms, *Nei Kung* and pushing hands drills.

These Five Steps are each identified with one of the Five Elements. Earth is in the centre, as the other Elements are to be found in or on it, just as the other Steps spring from Centrally Fixed. This is also a reason for the division of pushing hands into Fixed Step and Moving Step. In Tai Chi Chuan we train both to be able to step freely and to stand in a fixed position. In the latter method we do not step in any direction, although the feet may turn and we may switch the weight back and forward, changing from one stance into another. So, for example, where we had no room to step if we were attacked, we would employ body evasion rather than footwork.

The collective name for the *Ba Jin* and *Wu Bu* is the *Shi San Shi*. This term is usually translated as the Thirteen Postures or Movements, but I feel that in this context, the Thirteen Tactics is a better translation.

As has already been discussed, both the *Jin* and the *Bu* can be used in a number of ways, and so there is no limit to the possible permutations and combinations; as a result there are many more than just forty-eight self-defence exercises. The Five Steps and Eight Forces are not separate entities, but are drilled together in all aspects of Tai Chi Chuan. Their practical application lies in simultaneously evading and diverting an attack, and simultaneously closing with and countering the opponent.

The Practical Application of The Thirteen Tactics

The Classic of Tai Chi Chuan says:

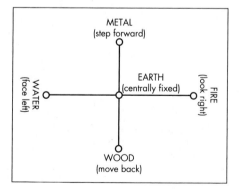

Fig 47　The Five Elements and the Five Steps.

Through practice (with a partner), we gradually perceive what it means to understand *Jin*.
From understanding *Jin* we can aspire to the highest level of ability.
However, we must exert ourselves over a long period of time
We can't suddenly become expert.

When the opponent is not in physical contact, the eyes must be used to detect his movements and feed the relevant information to the brain, which then, through the medium of the nervous system, instructs the body how to respond. Sometimes body evasion or footwork may be used; sometimes intercepting, redirecting or closing down on the opponent's technique; sometimes using a pre-emptive strike or throw of our own. However, the situation is quite different when we are in actual physical contact with an opponent: we are then too close to rely solely on the eyes to detect changes in the opponent's movements and instead must use *Ting Jin*, which literally means 'to listen for force', and by extension 'to be attentive' or 'to

obey'. The listening ability detects what the opponent is doing at the earliest possible stage so that, as before, his force can be redirected. This redirection is called *Hua Jin* and literally means 'to change' or 'transform'; by extension it can be interpreted as both a force (*Jin*) used to divert, and to divert (*Hua*) a force (*Jin*). The final

Fig 49　Hua Jin.

Fig 48　Ting Jin.

Fig 50　Fa Jin.

step is to *Fa Jin*: Fa means to shoot an arrow, and by extension means 'any expansion/ manifestation of latent energy'; so here it is simply to discharge force to counter an opponent. *Ting, Hua* and *Fa* skills are trained in pushing hands drills.

To sum up: when *not* in contact with an opponent:

1. Look for the opponent's *Jin*; then, in making contact:

2. Use *Jin* to redirect the opponent's Jin (*Hua Jin*)
3. Issue *Jin* to counter the opponent (*Fa Jin*)

When in contact with an opponent:

1. Listen for the opponent's *Jin* (*Ting Jin*);
2. Use *Jin* to redirect the opponent's *Jin* (*Hua Jin*);
3. Issue *Jin* to counter the opponent (*Fa Jin*).

7 Tui Shou (Pushing Hands)

'Pushing hands' is a direct translation of the Chinese term *Tui Shou*. In fact it is a misleading and unhelpful name for a wide variety of training drills which are used in Tai Chi Chuan, misleading because most of these drills involve considerably more than pushing, and the techniques used are not always restricted to hand movements.

Each style of Tai Chi Chuan has its particular pushing hands drills. There are certain drills such as the mistitled *Da Lu* which appear in various guises in most styles; others are particular to individual styles. All are designed to train co-ordination, footwork, balance, distance and timing. Some drills such as the Reeling Silk Pushing Hands additionally train a particular concept or skill.

To return to the name: some authorities state that *Tui Shou* was originally called *Ka Shou* or *Da Shou*. *Ka* means 'to scrape' or 'grate', so we would have scraping or grating hands; while *Da* means 'to strike' or 'to hit', so *Da Shou* is 'striking hands' – but a striking hand also alludes to a fighter in Chinese. Indeed, one of the Tai Chi Chuan classics, the *Da Shou Ge*, is often translated as the *Song of Pushing Hands*; although to be more accurate it should be translated as the *Song of Striking Hands* or the *Fighters' Song*. I believe that people

confused *Da Shou* and 'pushing hands' because they didn't know the fighting side of the art, and because they imagined that the *Fighters' Song* was only talking about pushing hands.

Logically, the exercises which are now referred to as 'pushing hands' were developed *after* the applications to enhance skills that would be useful in fighting, such as controlling an opponent at close quarters so that his vital points could be attacked. Subsequently, as is the case today, some people learned only the pushing hands drills, and not how to apply the skills thus acquired: so the drills became an end in themselves, a kind of pointless, unscripted, partnered ballet. Thus many people practised pushing hands, while few did the *San Shou* – literally 'Scattering Hands' – which is the term used to refer to self-defence techniques. So gradually, many practitioners came to perceive *Tui Shou* as a separate entity, which, coupled with knowledge of the form, would give them a self-defence capability. This is not so, however.

What do the drills involve? First, they train you to 'listen' for the opponent's *Jin* or force. 'Listening' is Tai Chi terminology for feeling what the other person is doing. Second, they train you in using *Jin* to divert or neutralize the opponent's attempts to use pull or push *Jin*. Third, they train you to discharge *Jin* against the opponent. *Jin* is essentially 'educated force', or 'force with technique'.

Pushing hands drills are methods of using the *Ba Jin* (Eight Forces) and the Five Steps; they are to be found in different combinations in the various pushing hands drills. Together the Eight Forces and Five Steps are referred to as the Thirteen Tactics, and governing their use we have the Five Strategies (all of which are discussed in the previous chapter).

PUSHING HANDS DRILLS

In addition to free and competition pushing hands, there are eight major methods of pushing hands drills and a number of auxiliary ones such as single hand pushing hands which are not quite as important. They can essentially be divided into two classes: fixed step and moving step.

Fixed Step Pushing Hands

Fu Yang means 'bow down, look up' and is designed to train the stance and the flexibility of the waist; as one partner bends forwards in a front stance to press on the other's torso, the other bends back and looks up, then as the partner's hands slide down his body he sinks and bends at the waist in a back stance.

Four Directions Pushing Hands is the most versatile drill of all. The four directions refer to the four cardinal points of the compass, and are identified with four ways of using *Jin*: *Peng* (upward diversion), *Lu* (sideways diversion), *Ji* (straight push) and *An* (downward push), each of which in turn is identified with the trigrams *Chien*, *Kun*, *Kan* and *Li*.

Fig 51   Sifus Tse Siu-chun and Lee Lai-ping demonstrating Fu Yang.

Fig 52   Four Directions Pushing Hands.

Using Four Directions we can move into many self-defence drills, including locking, trapping and sweeping. In addition the pattern of the Four Directions drill can be changed by stepping forwards and back and occasionally doing one push instead of two.

Reeling Silk Pushing Hands is training in a concept, the idea being called Gyrating Arms. As the opponent presses down or up on your arm with his, you follow the direction of his force and bring your arm round in an arc to counter-attack. This is the idea expressed in the classics of using 4oz of force to displace 1,000lb. The analogy of Reeling Silk refers to doing the technique smoothly, because if silk is jerked when being reeled from a cocoon it will break.

Fig 54   Sifus Lee Yim-ping and Lee Chun-sing demonstrate Single Hands Pushing Hands.

Zhou Lu pushing hands involves using the forearm or elbow to divert and lock the opponent's arm. I do not intend to show it here.

Single Hands Pushing Hands is one of the auxiliary methods of pushing hands used to train the stance and waist: as one partner gives by bringing his weight forwards and pushing the other's arm, the other receives by bringing his weight back and turning his waist.

Moving Step Pushing Hands

Moving step pushing hands also involves four major drills: Four Corners, Seven Stars, Nine Palaces and the Uprooting Wave.

Four Corners Step Pushing Hands is better known as *Da Lu* or Great Sideways Diversion, but this is not the correct name nor is it particularly helpful. The Four

Fig 53.   Reeling Silk Pushing Hands.

Fig 55   Lee Yim-ping and Tse Siu-chun demonstrate Da Lu.

Fig 56   Seven Stars Step Pushing Hands.

Corners are the four methods of using force called *Cai* (uproot), *Lie* (spiral), *Zhou* (elbow/ forearm technique), and *Kao* (shoulder/body technique). These are normally done diagonally and so are identified respectively with the trigrams *Sun*, *Chen*, *Tui* and *Ken*.

The other name for the Four Corners is Eight Gates and Five Steps. The Eight Gates are the Eight Trigrams, and the Five Steps are, of course, Forward, Back, Left, Right and Central Equilibrium. This is also a reference to the Thirteen Tactics. You can go through the Eight Gates or eight points of the compass in turn when doing Four Corners, or you can do it in a much freer manner. As in other pushing hands, as one goes forwards and pushes, the other goes back and diverts.

Seven Stars Step Pushing Hands consists of seven sliding steps forward combined with seven pushes in a zig-zag pattern, matched by seven steps back and seven diversions. The Seven Stars refer to the

Great Bear, or the Dipper, and this is a common Taoist reference. A number of variations can also be employed. Linked to techniques from the form, the weapons and *Nei Kung*, it trains the ability to evade and counter-attack.

Nine Palaces Step Pushing Hands also trains evasion and counter-attack, but here the pusher crosses his legs as he does two pushes, while his partner steps back twice to divert; they then change roles. The Nine Palaces refer to the Eight Trigrams and the centre, the Tai Chi. A number of variations can also be employed in this method of pushing hands, to produce a spiral, an uprooting, to change the lead leg, for example. This method can also be used when practising Sticking Spears.

Fig 57   Sticking Spears with Nine Palaces Step.

Fig 58   My first student Michael Jacques on his way to winning the British Open Tai Chi Championships Heavyweight Pushing Hands title in 1993.

The Uprooting Wave (*Cai Lang*) Pushing Hands is the most advanced of all the eight methods, and its concepts of wave-like motion and the use of total body force can be adapted to fit into the other methods of pushing hands; it can also be applied to self defence, form, Nei Kung and weapons training. Sometimes it is incorrectly referred to as Lan Cai Hua or Orchid Flower. It has many possible variations, and can be done as a fixed step method; normally, however, it is done with moving step. Again, I don't intend to show it here.

Free and Competitive Pushing Hands

I first heard of pushing hands competitions in about 1977. Free pushing hands, where one tries to push or pull the opponent off balance, has long been considered by Tai Chi exponents as a genuine test of skill as it involves grappling skills, and the ability to redirect the opponent's force and to *Fa Jin*, or to use force at close quarters. The major problem with free pushing hands is the rules. First of all, should fixed step or moving step be used? In fixed step, the first to step out of his stance is the loser. Moving step is generally done in an area such as a large circle, and the loser is the first to fall in it or to be pushed out of it. Then there is restricted step, where under certain conditions, the competitors can take a sliding step forwards or back.

What techniques should be allowed in free or competitive pushing hands? Many of my Tai Chi colleagues will say in reply: '*Peng, Lu, Ji, An, Cai, Lie, Zhou, Kao* combined with Step Forward, Step Back, Step Left, Step Right and Central Equilibrium.' However, it is unlikely that Chang San-feng awoke one morning with the brilliant idea of creating a martial art from eight techniques based on the *Ba Gua* – the Eight Trigrams and five types of footwork based on the Five Elements. More probable is that Tai Chi Chuan is the Yin Yang theory made martial, and that these eight methods of using force were a subsequent development, distilled from an analysis of the already existing Tai Chi self-defence techniques.

Looking at the self-defence techniques, we can see that many of them do not fit neatly into any of the eight afore-mentioned categories, nor is the distinction between these eight categories always entirely clear. Their value is that they do help us to understand and train in methods of using force, and such training is largely done in pushing hands drills. So, what is to be allowed in free or competitive pushing hands? Will pulling be allowed? If not, why not? As a number of Tai Chi self-defence techniques incorporate pulling, it seems strange not to permit it. The more restrictions there are, the more difficult is the task of the officials, the more frustrating the competition for competitors as they are always being pulled up by the referee, the more boring the competition for the spectators, and the less it is a real test of martial skills.

Some people complain that pushing hands competitions are no way to test martial ability. In the case of certain types of competition this is true, but the basic purpose of freestyle or competition pushing hands should be to get the opponent off balance. This is a crucial close-quarters fighting skill which sets up situations for throws, locks and strikes, and one which many practitioners of primarily striking arts such as karate or taekwondo do not possess. It is one of the main reasons why many of these practitioners

take up arts such as Tai Chi Chuan, which do train this type of skill. I found these skills most useful as a police officer in Hong Kong, and I am at present imparting them to security guard trainees. Once you understand the key concepts of 'listening' for, and then redirecting and discharging force, it becomes much easier to control an arrested person, without necessarily having to whack him, although that remains an option.

Some Tai Chi practitioners are competent in pushing hands, but are still not martial artists. Since 1991 I have attended the *Rencontres Jasnières* Tai Chi camp as an instructor, and many of my students have also attended. In the afternoons, three hours are devoted to free pushing hands. You can push with anyone for up to ten minutes before changing partners or taking a break.

On the final day of the camp in 1991, I was asked to push hands with one of the top French instructors. After a bit I asked him why he kept withdrawing one of his hands, and he told me it was so that he could use it suddenly to shove or pull. I replied that pushing hands was about training listening ability, and that if he didn't have contact he couldn't listen, nor could he control my free hand which I would therefore use to strike him. His rejoinder was that he was a soccer player not a martial artist, and that his teacher in Taiwan had told him that pushing hands training alone was enough for him to defend himself. In fairness I have to admit that he was pretty good at pushing hands.

There is a degree of etiquette involved in pushing hands, so that if wrestling or striking techniques are to be allowed, this should be agreed beforehand; unfortunately some people get a bit too enthusiastic at times. For instance, in my

Fig 59   The author teaching pushing hands at the *Rencontres Jasnières* camp.

the shoulder, thanked him and walked away. The same gentleman tried the same method against one of the American instructors the next day and they ended up rolling around the grass until the American eventually managed to pin my friend.

In one of my first Tai Chi classes, a young lady who had been brought along by one of my students was doing free pushing hands, but was having problems with it. After I'd explained how to do it and why we did it, she said, 'What if he does this?' and simultaneously kicked at my groin. Fortunately I caught her leg and threw her fairly gently. I was later told that she felt she really needed to be thrown, also that she was undergoing psychotherapy. The bottom line is, don't expect the nice gentleman or lady with whom you are pushing hands to push hands *your* way; but expect the unexpected. This is what pushing hands and listening are about: if people take, or attempt to take liberties, they should not be surprised if this is reciprocated.

I don't want my students to be surprised or hurt; that is why I teach pushing hands as part of an integrated system, and link it from the beginning to the self-defence and grappling applications.

second year at *Rencontres Jasnières* a large Englishman from the Cheng Man-ching school asked to push hands with me. We made contact, and he immediately grabbed my legs to try to take me down. Not wishing to dirty my expensive clothes, I hit him in the face with my forearm, breaking his glasses. After drawing this fact to my attention, he continued to push with me with great enthusiasm but with little success, until I patted him on

8 San Shou
(Self Defence)

Many people believe that the self-defence applications in Tai Chi Chuan come from the hand form. This is ridiculous, yet we have photographs of Yang Cheng-fu, for example, doing self-defence applications with precisely the same postures as he used when demonstrating his hand form. Perhaps because of his size he did not find it convenient to side step, but few of his applications are practical and they do not follow the Tai Chi theory of using 4oz against 1,000lb of force. Perhaps he was hiding the true applications, or perhaps he'd just forgotten them.

The hand form – in fact any form in any martial art – is merely a blend of existing techniques adapted to follow a certain sequence. This sequence is usually important in itself, as one technique is often linked to the next. The techniques which make up the hand form are part of the repertoire of *Tai Chi San Shou*, but their application often requires modification in the form of footwork and changing

Fig 60   Grasping Bird's Tail (Lower Level).

Fig 61   Break Arm Style.

Fig 62   Pat Horse High.

Figs 63   Cross Hands.

The term *San Shou* is often not clearly explained. *San* originally meant 'to cut meat into filaments by striking it'. It then came to mean to 'scatter' or 'break up'. *Shou* means 'hand' or 'hands'. Thus *Tai Chi San Shou* is a method of dissipating or dispersing the opponent's attacks and countering him. Some styles of Tai Chi Chuan have *San Shou* forms which are also sometimes referred to as 'two person sets': a choreographed series of attacks and responses done in a manner similar to pushing hands. However, while these are fun to do, I believe that it is more important to practise repeated variations on, and responses to, individual techniques or combinations of techniques.

Some people say that it takes ten or twenty years before one can use Tai Chi Chuan to defend oneself, and they are right: the *San Shou* and related martial training offered by many Tai Chi schools is so deficient or unrealistic that it is doubtful if the techniques could ever be used in a practical situation. In addition, few Tai Chi Chuan teachers have the practical knowledge of fighting against other styles, or of street self defence.

THE SCIENCE OF FIGHTING

At this stage it is appropriate to investigate how to apply some of the techniques learned in previous chapters (namely Strategies and Tactics, and Pushing Hands).

Position, Timing and Distance

To develop effective self-defence abilities, it is not enough to learn techniques by rote: it is also important to learn how and when to apply them in different

the angle. Forty-eight major techniques, mostly, from the hand form, and another sixteen of the twenty-four *Nei Kung* exercises have self-defence applications, most of which can be done in more than one way and in different combinations.

145

situations. There is a certain science to this, and the three key principles are position, timing and distance. Successful self defence requires mastery of these three aspects.

Position

The position of the body and of the hands is of paramount importance when facing an attacker, when evading an attack, and when counter-attacking. As far as possible the hands should be in front of the body and the body should face the opponent, but not square on. Failure to secure the correct angle will result in any counter made being much less effective, particularly where faced with more than one opponent, or in the case of counters involving the use of grappling techniques. As far as angle is concerned, the normal aim will be to manipulate the opponent's centre line by evasion, or by diversion of his attack or otherwise so that he is not in a good position to follow up his initial

Fig 65   Good positioning: the defender can see both opponents.

attack, and that he is in a suitable position for our counter. The corollary is that, having evaded or redirected his attack, our own centre line should normally be facing the opponent so as to conveniently follow up with our counter.

Distance

The *Tai Chi Chuan Canon (Ching)* states:

> Now conceal, now reveal your intentions,
> When there is pressure on the left, then make the left empty.
> When there is pressure on the right, then make the right distant.
> When the opponent looks up, I am still higher;
> When he looks down, I am still lower.
> When he advances, the distance seems surpassingly long;
> When he retreats the distance seems surpassingly short.
> A feather cannot be added,
> A fly cannot land.
> Nobody knows me,

Fig 64   Bad positioning: the defender cannot see the second opponent.

I alone know them.
An invincible hero can thus be made.
All this is achieved in the same way.

In genuine self-defence situations there is often no opportunity to assume an 'on guard' position; but it is necessary to respond immediately to the assailant's aggression. The aim should be to redirect the opponent's attack and therefore his body into empty air – the void. At the same time the defender positions his body and hands so that he is ready and able to proceed with a counter-attack. The same result can be achieved by side-stepping, or using body evasion instead of, or allied to, a diversion of the attack.

A guard is often a useful method for the defender to control the distance between him and his opponent: the longer the distance between, the more time he has to react to his attack. A guard can also be used in other ways, for example a low guard can be used to tempt the opponent to attack high, or vice versa.

He can also maintain the distance. If the opponent tries to bridge the intervening gap he can respond by moving back to the same extent as the opponent moves forwards so that the distance is effectively maintained. As the defender goes back he redirects his attack/s, and before he can continue, suddenly closes the gap to make his counter. Exercises such as Seven Star Step Pushing Hands are fundamental to training this type of skill.

Whether stepping back, forwards, or to the side, it is important to do so in order to evade effectively, but still close enough to make our counter.

The reference to the distance being surpassingly long or short can be expressed by the phrase 'Retreat in order to advance', a concept from Chinese

Fig 66–70 Moving back out of range of opponent's attack, then moving in with Fair Lady Works at Shuttle to spiral his attack back into him.

military strategy: we retreat out of range, then close the distance to counter-attack.

Timing
Tai Chi theory states that:

> If the opponent doesn't move,
> I don't move,
> If the opponent moves even a little,
> I move first.
> Appear relaxed, but don't be flaccid.
> Be prepared to move but don't move.

Essentially Tai Chi Chuan is a counter-attacking system, so the defender doesn't generally attack first, but prefers to wait for the opponent to commit himself to a course of action; he can then detect this action at the earliest possible stage and counter him. Sometimes the counter will require defence to be used, then attack; on other occasions a pre-emptive strike is better. Sometimes the defender has to provoke the opponent into attacking: he can crowd him and close his space down, or use feints to draw his sting. As soon as he reacts, the defender must be able to respond with an appropriate counter.

There are three levels of timing:

a) After the technique is on, when the defender is only aware of the opponent's attack after he has been hit or grabbed by him. This is the lowest level of ability.

b) When the technique is on, where the

Fig 71 Beating the opponent to the punch.

defender only manages to react at a late stage to an attack; sometimes he will be successful in countering the opponent, sometimes not.

c) Before the technique is on, where the defender detects the opponent's intentions at the earliest possible stage and is able to counter him with ease.

In addition the defender may evade the opponent in situations b) or c) above, but this good work is wasted unless he immediately counter-attacks. This is the meaning of the saying in the *Fighters' Song* 'The *Jin* [force] is broken; the intent is unbroken'.

Moving at the appropriate speed is also important. The *Tai Chi Chuan Canon* says:

> If the opponent's actions are swift, then my response is swift.
> If his actions are slow then I follow him slowly.

Xin, *Yi* and Focus

Xin literally means 'heart', and in the Tai Chi Chuan classics it is used to mean 'the mind'. So in the Tai Chi Chuan classics it is written, 'First in the mind, then in the body'. And 'The mind acts as the commander; the *Qi* acts as the flag; the waist acts as the banner.'

Yi has a slightly different meaning, corresponding to 'intent' or 'purpose'. This is of great importance in self defence and is trained in forms and pushing hands. The intent is seen in the eyes which should normally be looking at where the technique is going. One of the key phrases appended to the *Da Shou Ge* (*Fighters' Song*) is, 'The *Jin* [technique] is broken, but the *Yi* [intent] is unbroken.' This statement can be considered in two ways. First, the defender must maintain his intent to defeat his opponent, and be

prepared to follow up his technique, whether defensive or offensive. Second, it is not usually enough simply to defend against the opponent's initial attack, but we must immediately counter him, otherwise he will almost certainly have the intent to attack again. To sum up, effective self defence depends upon the defender maintaining intent, and destroying or removing the intent of the opponent. These concepts are strongly related to the five close-quarter strategies, which we have discussed.

Focus is talking about correct alignment. Generally the eyes, the nose, the centre line of the body and the hand/s and knee/s should be pointing in the same direction when we strike an opponent who is in front of us. Focus is important from an aesthetic point of view, in that it makes forms look more meaningful and martial; however, its main importance is that a focused technique is much more powerful as the whole body's force and weight are being used, rather than just the strength of the striking arm or leg.

The essence of Tai Chi self defence and forms is circle and focus: one Yin and one Yang.

PUTTING THEORY INTO PRACTICE

How is all this theory best related to actual daily practice? Pushing hand drills are practised to give skills in footwork, listening, following, balance, grappling, stance and so on, all of which are useful in self defence. Most of the self-defence techniques which are used in Tai Chi Chuan are practised in the form, but not in the same way that they are actually used: this is because the form lacks the necessary footwork and body evasion, and techniques have been rounded off for aesthetic purposes or to disguise them.

The form is, however, a method *par excellence* of training the concept of total body force, a concept which plays a major part in making the techniques effective. Other key skills such as co-ordination, intent and focus are trained in the form in equal measure. Refining the technique also produces what is referred to as 'fine work, neatly done', so that the opponent finds it difficult to penetrate. In other words, if techniques are clumsy and too big, as is often the case with beginners, openings are created which an opponent can exploit. Further, not only does the form incorporate individual techniques, it also gives combinations for situations where one is faced with more than one opponent, or where one technique is resisted or doesn't work and so must immediately be followed with another. This again brings in the concepts of *Yi* (intent) and *Sui* (following), covered earlier.

The twelve *Yin* and twelve *Yang* exercises of *Tai Chi Nei Kung* have many dimensions to them, including training the use of *Jin*, refining technique and developing a calm mind. The *Yin* exercises energize the body enabling the defender to receive force – to withstand an opponent's blows as well as to recover from injury – while the *Yang* exercises are more for increasing muscular power and the ability to *Fa Jin*, or discharge force. Like the form techniques, these exercises can be linked together or with techniques of the form to produce yet more variations. Furthermore, Tai Chi Chuan weapons training gives other ways of

Fig 72   The author's first-round knockout of Roy Pink in the Open Weight Division of the 5th South-East Asian Chinese Martial Arts Championships in Malaysia, April 1980.

educating and exercising the body, and incorporates kicks, grabs and strikes in the applications.

As well as all these methods of skill training, if Tai Chi Chuan is to be used for self defence, it is advisable to do Tai Chi Chuan conditioning training, that is, the Yang aspects for power and stamina. This is an area often neglected by martial artists in general and Tai Chi practitioners in particular, in the mistaken belief that technique alone is enough. Few people have the aptitude or the time to acquire a high skill level quickly. It takes four to six months to give someone the basic conditioning to do full contact fighting, ie to be able to withstand blows and to knock out an opponent with one strike. It takes a lot longer to acquire a high level of technique, so if you wish to be able to defend yourself adequately or to fight full contact, there should be an emphasis on conditioning training from the beginning.

To sum up, those with neither skill nor power cannot fight. Those who have some skill, but who lack timing, power, stamina and the ability to receive force will always be in a dangerous situation. Those who have timing, power, stamina and the ability to receive force will be able to defeat most opponents. Those who, in addition, possess a clear mind, together with a knowledge of all the theoretical and practical aspects of Tai Chi Chuan, can be considered Tai Chi Chuan fighters.

9 Weapons and Other Equipment

The three traditional Tai Chi weapons of spear, sabre and sword are normally taught to students once a certain degree of ability has been acquired in other aspects of the art. Just as with the hand techniques, so with the weapons there are particular *Jin* and stepping methods attached.

Why learn weapons? First, they are excellent methods of exercise with jumping, spinning, kicking and juggling skills which help educate the body in coordination, focus and the use of force. Second, if you are faced with a weapon, it is useful to be able to pick up an everyday object such as a length of wood or an umbrella and use it to defend yourself. Third, through weapons training you become used to moving and attempting to defend yourself when holding something in your hand. Finally, the weapons are a traditional part of the art, so for the sake of completeness we should know them.

SPEAR, SABRE AND SWORD

There is a saying in Chinese martial arts: 'Spear one hundred days; sabre one thousand days, sword ten thousand days.' Essentially this means that the spear form is relatively short and so can be learned fairly quickly, though mastery is another thing. It requires the use of both hands to hold and manipulate the spear. The practice weapon should be tapered at the stabbing end which enables it to vibrate when Jin is applied through it, making the opponent lose control of his weapon when he makes contact with it. Ideally the spear should be from eight to nine feet in length, although for demonstration purposes it should be from seven to eight feet in length with a metal head and a piece of red cloth attached to the neck. It is primarily a stabbing weapon.

The sabre is a practical and relatively easy-to-use weapon, though the form is much longer than the spear form. When cradled in the left hand and held point down, it should be just short of touching the floor. Dragon Well sabres from China are the best balanced. The form contains a lot of kicking techniques, and the other hand is used to grab the opponent's body or weapon. The sabre is primarily for slashing and chopping.

As regards swords, Dragon Well are again the best make. The sword should stand about three inches lower than the height of the navel. The index and middle fingers of the spare hand are extended as if to make a miniature sword, and are used as a reference point for the position of the sword or to strike the opponent's

Fig 73   Sifu Cheng Kam with Tai Chi spear.

Fig 75   Sifu Lau Lai-kwan demonstrating Golden Dragon Coiled Round a Pillar.

Fig 74   Sweeping across a Thousand Troops.

vital points. Again there are many kicking techniques to be used when the sword is engaged with the opponent's weapon. The sword is primarily a stabbing and slicing weapon.

The sword form is the longest and most elaborate of the weapon forms. The sword was the weapon of the *literati* and the officer class. Indeed, Li Bai, the great poet, wrote that at fifteen he already loved the sword – and later he was to kill with it, not once, but several times.

PRACTISING THE FORMS

The forms in the system which I practise are comparatively gymnastic and martial (though the sword form can be done more slowly), whereas in most others they tend to be very slow and stylized. This suggests that someone after the time of Yang Lu-chan made the forms in these other styles more gentle to suit the clientele. I have discussed key concepts in practising hand form; most of these also apply to weapon forms, save that softness is not entirely appropriate. Although the three tradition-al weapon forms all have a soft beginning and end, all require discharging *Jin* through the weapon thus making it vibrate (this does not apply to wooden swords and sabres).

Spear techniques can be applied with everyday objects such as rakes and brooms, while sword and sabre tech-niques can be applied with a short umbrella, police baton or even rolled-up newspaper. The method of application includes the Yin Yang theory of evasion

153

and counter-attack we discussed in the section on self defence, as well as the use of kicking and grabbing techniques while at close quarters.

Many styles have some pattern of two person weapon sparring, following a set routine. Certainly some form of weapon sparring or application is important, both to understand the techniques of the weapon forms and to execute them correctly.

OTHER WEAPONS AND FORMS

Other weapons are used in certain Tai Chi systems; for instance, in the rare Hao style there is a form with a short sword. There are double sword forms, though I believe this came from the influence of *Ba Gua*, as this art appeared in Beijing with the arrival of Dong Hai-chuan, a contemporary of Yang Lu-chan. Dong was also appointed as an instructor of martial arts in the Forbidden City.

More recently, new forms with single and double fans and walking-sticks have been devised. The walking-stick form incorporates techniques borrowed from Western fencing as well as traditional Chinese weapon techniques. In my opinion these forms are less practical than the traditional ones, though they can be fun to do. And there is also the Tai Chi whip, which is a rattan cane or stick.

Another unusual piece of equipment is the Tai Chi ruler, which is not used as a ruler at all, but as a form of soft exercise or *Qi Gong*. This again is fairly recent. One of my Tai Chi elder brothers in Hong Kong is an authority on it, though it is not part of the syllabus of our school.

Fig 76   Sifus Lee Yim-ping and Lee Chung-ling with Tai Chi fan.

TAI CHI BALLS

There are also Tai Chi balls which are popular. Before World War II a certain Tai Chi instructor invented an exercise method using large balls which resembled the medicine balls of Western boxing in size and weight; however, it didn't catch on. The so-called Tai Chi balls (they have little to do with Tai Chi Chuan except for the name) are much smaller, they have bells inside them, and they are used to exercise the hands to prevent arthritis.

I don't find any of these methods very interesting compared with the traditional ones. I prefer to spend more time doing mirror image forms with the weapons instead, because I believe that as a professional you should be able to teach southpaws as easily as anyone else and be able to defend yourself with either hand.

10 Heal or Hurt

PHYSIOLOGICAL ASPECTS OF TAI CHI CHUAN

Both my parents are doctors, and I believe this has given me a uniquely jaundiced view of the dark science of medicine and those who practise it. It is worth considering that while an individual may be entitled to call himself 'doctor' as a result of graduating bottom of his medical class thirty years previously from some obscure university, this hardly puts him in the best position to provide his patients with treatment using the cutting edge of new technology. As far as traditional Chinese medicine and alternative medicine are concerned, the picture is murkier still. At least with a properly qualified Western doctor you are sure that he has a certain basic knowledge and training. Often in Chinese stories and films there is the character of the itinerant traditional Chinese doctor, and one of the reasons that some of these gentlemen *were* itinerant was so that they weren't around to suffer retribution at the hands of dissatisfied patients.

Doctors on the whole take a dim view of martial arts injuries – 'it's your own fault' – and often advise complete rest. In fact such advice is not only unhelpful and complacent, but in some instances it is woefully wrong. Fortunately a few enlightened practitioners are more open-minded about the benefits of exercise, and there are some sports medicine clinics doing a good job.

One of my students, Dr Mike Webb, is a medical researcher: while helping me to research some material on the Tai Chi Chuan classics and specifically the concept of the *Qi* entering the bones, he came across some interesting studies on exercise in general, and Tai Chi Chuan in particular, and the effect these had on the body. The first study was made at the Human Nutrition Research Center on Ageing at Tufts University, Boston, Maryland, and concerned thirty-nine post-menopausal, sedentary, estrogen-deplete white women aged from fifty to seventy years of age: twenty women were given five different high-intensity strength-training exercises two days per week for one year, while the other group went untreated. The study found that muscle mass, muscle strength and dynamic balance increased while bone density was preserved in the strength-trained group, but that all these factors decreased in the untreated group.

Next was a study over two years of a twenty-six year old female by the Bone Research Group, UKK Institute, Tampere,

Finland. It found that physical training has the potential to increase the mass of healthy bones, whereas immobilization, when used as a treatment of soft tissue and bone injuries, is shown to result in atrophy of these tissues.

There was also a study of the effects of resistance training on prepubescent children. For twelve weeks fifty-two children were given the training, which consisted of maximum sustained isometric contraction of elbow flexion for ten seconds. A control group of forty-seven children did not receive the training. After the twelve weeks, both groups showed increases in the cross-sectional areas of tissue in the upper arm; however, in the control group this was because of an increase in fat area, while in the training group it was due to increases in muscle and bone area.

Finally an American review found that part of the reduction in bone density observed in older people is due to disuse rather than the ageing process itself, and that older people who have been active for many years seem to exhibit generally enhanced bone density.

The following specifically Tai Chi-based studies were also conducted: first, the Department of Physical Medicine and Rehabilitation at the National Taiwan University Hospital treated a group of forty-one males and females aged from fifty to sixty-four years, and a control group of forty-nine sedentary males and females. Tests found that the oxygen uptake, O2 pulse and work rate of the Tai Chi group were significantly higher than those of the control group.

At the University of Connecticut, School of Medicine, in a study of women aged sixty-two to seventy-five years, those who did only posture control exercises, including some simple Tai Chi exercises, showed no significant difference in improved posture compared with a control group who did these exercises and some flexibility training as well – in other words, there is as much benefit to be had from Tai Chi alone in terms of improved posture, as from Tai Chi plus flexibility training.

The Department of Health Sports and Leisure Studies at the North-Eastern University in Boston compared the metabolic and cardio-respiratory responses to the continuous performance of Wing Chun and Tai Chi Chuan exercise. The study found that the ventilatory equivalent for oxygen obtained during Tai Chi Chuan exercise was significantly lower than for Wing Chun exercise, suggesting that 'Tai Chi practitioners utilize efficient breathing patterns during exercise'. However, the study also found that only the continuous performance of Wing Chun exercise elicited values for oxygen uptake and heart-rate responses that would be expected to bring about a cardio-respiratory training effect in subjects with a relatively low initial value of oxygen uptake.

One of the problems with the last study is, what do we mean by 'continuous practice of Wing Chun and Tai Chi Chuan exercise'? Both these arts have hard and soft elements, and there are many different approaches to both arts. For example, typical Cheng Man-ching hand form is very understated, while other styles like my own are somewhat more vigorous and expansive. The vigorous and continuous practice of Tai Chi spear or Tai Chi throwing techniques would definitely cause a cardio-respiratory training effect, while the ventilatory equivalent for oxygen would certainly be higher.

Since 1975, my own experiences with

Tai Chi Chuan tend to confirm these studies. First, a number of asthmatic students have been able to abandon their inhalers. Diabetic students have found improvements in their metabolism, making it unnecessary to take so much insulin. Students with bad backs and joint problems have also found improvements, particularly through the *Nei Kung* exercises. Tai Chi Chuan has also helped those with digestive problems, including kidney disorders; and a number of students who suffered from insomnia have confirmed to me that Nei Kung training has helped them.

TAI CHI CHUAN BREATHING

There are many theories about breathing, circulation and the concept of *Qi*. Many Tai Chi Chuan teachers say you should breathe naturally, but what is natural? The tip of the tongue should make contact with the roof of the mouth just behind the front teeth to aid salivation. The production and swallowing of saliva is extremely beneficial as saliva has considerable antiseptic qualities which help with digestion and prevent stomach ulcers and bad breath. The mouth should be closed, and breathing should be in and out through the nose because the nose filters and warms the air before it is taken into the lungs. If instead you breathe in through the mouth you will feel the air to be cold, infections such as colds will be contracted more easily, and the mouth and throat will very quickly become dry and uncomfortable. In addition, breathing through the nose makes the action of breathing smoother and more even.

From a martial point of view there are other benefits of breathing through the nose and keeping the mouth closed: for instance, if you are hit on the jaw with the mouth open it is more likely that you will have a broken jaw or bite your tongue than if the mouth were closed. Furthermore at close quarters it is a common ploy in Chinese martial arts to attack when the opponent is breathing in, and as nasal breathing is quieter than breathing through the mouth, it is more difficult for the opponent to exploit such opportunities.

When performing the hand form and other aspects of Tai Chi Chuan, the breathing should follow the movements. Some instructors say that you should breathe *out* when doing an expansive or opening movement – that is, when the limbs are raised or extended outwards – and *in* when doing a contracting or closing movement – when the limbs are lowered or retracted. Other instructors teach the converse of this, often termed reverse breathing. The former is more common, and if you forget about the breath and concentrate on the movements – as advised by the addendum to the Explanation to the Operation of the Thirteen Tactics – you will find yourself following this method most of the time. When pushing hands or fighting, we exhale when pushing, pulling, hitting, or throwing the opponent.

In Tai Chi Chuan there is the concept of abdominal breathing, introduced by phrases such as 'Let the *Qi* sink to the *Tan Tien*': if movements are soft and slow, we will be more relaxed. The diaphragm will be more flexible and thus the lungs will be able to extend further downwards, enabling us to take in more oxygen. The downward extension and upward contraction of the lungs are seen and felt in the lower abdomen, and act to massage the internal organs, thus aiding digestion and circulation.

There are many abstruse and arcane theories about breathing methods and Qi circulation in relation to both Tai Chi Chuan and *Qi Gong*, and it is useful to examine the origins of some of these theories and to assess their validity.

CHINESE ALCHEMY

The Chinese have, like the Americans, always been obsessed with longevity, what they called 'long life without ageing'. So how to achieve it? There were two ways: internal and external alchemy.

Wai Dan: External Alchemy

Joseph Needham translates this term as 'inorganic laboratory alchemy', as opposed to *Nei Dan* which he calls 'physiological alchemy'. He distinguishes the former as being concerned with elixir preparations of mineral origin, whereas the latter is concerned with operations within the human body. More simply, these two terms are often translated as respectively external alchemy and internal alchemy.

The *Dan* referred to in *Nei/Wai Dan* is the *Dan/Tan* of the *Dan/Tan Tian/Tien*, 'the cinnabar field', a point which every good martial artist knows is approximately two inches below the navel. The ancient form of this character is shown in Fig 77, and represents the crucible of the alchemist containing cinnabar. Cinnabar is mercuric sulphide, and was rated as the number one drug of all in Shen Nung's *Treatise on Medicine* completed during the Eastern Han dynasty (25–220 AD). It fascinated the Chinese alchemists for

Fig 77 Dan.

thousands of years, and they would heat it causing it to break down into sulphur dioxide and mercury. They would then combine the mercury again with sulphur, usually to make black metacinnabar which when heated could be transformed yet again, back to the original red cinnabar. So what did they do with it? They ate it to give themselves energy, including sexual energy; and they ate it to give themselves long life. Unfortunately mercury is poisonous, and too much makes you very dead. (My Tai Chi friends in Hong Kong use this character to address me!)

Since the Shang dynasty (c1500 BC) the Chinese have tried to find the elixir of life by eating cinnabar, ginseng and the bone marrow of human sacrifices. At the behest of Chinese friends, I have eaten ginseng, bear gall bladder, deer penis (pickled in brandy), dog and snake. The idea is that either the unique properties of the elixir or the effect of the elixir on the chemical processes of the body would lead to physical, mental and even spiritual benefits.

Even to this day, many Chinese and Westerners swear by all kinds of drugs, poisons, plants and potions. I found this out the hard way in 1976, when I was with the Hong Kong kung fu team for the South East Asian Full Contact Championships in Singapore. Sifu Chew Theng-ying, one of my Tai Chi uncles (now deceased), ran a herbalist store in Singapore. He provided me and my elder brother, Chow Kim-tong, with high quality ginseng to eat before the fights to give us more Yang energy. After a fight we had to eat papaya to balance the Yang with Yin. I was also offered anabolic steroids by one of the officials in the Hong Kong team – I refused to take them, but several team members took opium to calm their nerves before fighting.

I took a vicious pounding in the first fight against a powerful Malaysian, whom I stopped. So severe was the bruising that the tournament doctor insisted that I have a tetanus shot. The well known bone-setter, Sifu Tang Chi-kong, gave me a herbal mudpack for my left foot which had swollen to almost twice its normal size as a result of stamp kicks, and I took bear gall bladder for the internal bruising. In addition, Uncle Chew massaged my injuries, rubbing in white flower oil. All these applications can be termed 'Wai Dan'.

Nei Dan: Internal Alchemy

This is a controversial and badly misunderstood subject, but one which concerns us all as it deals with the ancient Taoist idea of trying to have a long life while avoiding the infirmities that come with age. Internal alchemy is governed by three forces: *Qi*, *Jing* and *Shen*, and the characters for these terms are replete with alchemical significance. All are mentioned in the Tai Chi Chuan classics, and we have seen some of the medical effects

Fig 78   Qui/Chi.

Fig 79   Jing.

of exercise in general and Tai Chi Chuan in particular, so we can say that Tai Chi Chuan is a type of internal alchemy.

The character for *Qi/Chi* is shown in Fig 78, and represents rice being cooked and giving off vapour. It can mean the breath, air, circulation, stamina, the character and lots more besides. In the context of internal alchemy perhaps the best translation of it is 'vital force'. (Note that this is not the same character as the *Chi* in Tai Chi Chuan.)

The character for *Jing* is shown in Fig 79 and represents rice or grain giving birth, and cinnabar. For our purposes, 'sexual energy' or 'vital essence' is

Fig 80   Shen.

probably the best equivalent in English. (Note this is a different character from the Jin/Jing which means 'force'.)

The character for Shen is shown in Fig 80; it gives the idea of expanding or extending and receiving the will of heaven or the gods as manifested by the changes of the sun, moon and stars in heaven. By extension, this term means 'spiritual essence'.

The Chinese see these three forces as being interrelated. Logically, if the respiratory and circulatory functions of the body are functioning inefficiently because of illness, stress, bad posture or some other cause, then the sexual functions and mental/spiritual functions are likely to be impaired. Likewise, if the mental/spiritual state is impaired due to emotional trauma, drug abuse or suchlike then breathing, circulation and sexual performance are also often adversely affected.

Tai Chi Chuan and Internal Alchemy

The brain needs to be supplied with blood (which contains Qi); the pituitary gland contains hormones which control the formation of sperm or ova in man and woman respectively; while the spinal cord – which is basically a continuation of the brain – controls the autonomic nervous system which regulates sexual (emission of Jing) functions and the release of drugs (adrenaline, acetyl choline and so on) and so is crucial to the regulation of internal alchemy. So, how to maximize the supply of Qi, of Jing, of Shen? Well, there are the external alchemy methods of drug and diet already alluded to, and there were also the methods of internal alchemy which arose out of Taoist philosophical and religious practices.

Where to get the best Qi? There are two possibilities. In the I Ching (Book of Changes), Yang is represented by an unbroken line (—) and Yin by a broken line (– –). These lines can also be seen in a sexual context, the unbroken line being the male penis, while the broken line is the vagina. Heaven and Earth are the supreme Yang and Yin forces and so were represented respectively by the trigrams Chien and Kun: where better to get cosmic Qi than in the misty mountains or in the bowels of the earth ? This is why, in the Zhou dynasty, certain emperors conducted banquets and orgies in underground chambers. It is also the reason for the premium prices paid by Chinese for wild animals which have a rich store of cosmic Qi from dwelling in burrows and sets.

Famous men travelled to sacred mountains, to places such as the Taoist retreat of Wudang Mountain, in order to meditate – often in caves or tree huts – and to exercise and study in the midst of Nature. It is no accident that Bodhidharma and Chang San-feng are respectively identified with the Zen Buddhist Shaolin temple on Mount Song and the Taoist temples on

Wudang Mountain and at Baoji. Dawn is the best time to seek cosmic *Qi*, when the plants are giving off oxygen and the air is clear. To this day in the early morning Chinese people can be found in parks embracing trees or exercising under them to draw their cosmic *Qi*.

Chinese martial arts are thousands of years old, as is the Chinese concept of Yin and Yang; also the idea of gentle exercise and massage as a means to health is well over 2,000 years old. Over the centuries these individual elements were synthesized to produce a subtle and sophisticated martial art which also possessed therapeutic, meditative and philosophical elements, a martial art that would prove popular with the intellectual elite and later with the masses: they called it Tai Chi Chuan. The Tai Chi Chuan classics also refer to these three forces; for instance, the *Song of The Thirteen Tactics* states:

> Internally, if the abdomen is relaxed and still, the *Qi* ascends.
> When the coccyx is straight, the *Shen* connects with the headtop.
> The whole body feels light and agile when the headtop is suspended.

In order to achieve this, it is necessary for our movements to be relaxed and natural and for the back to be straight. Western medical knowledge agrees with these ideas on the whole.

Developing *Qi* and *Jing*

There are hundreds of methods for training the breath and circulation, and multifarious variations of each method. Some of these are wrong, some right; some are beneficial, and some highly dangerous. The more *Qi* you had, potentially the more *Jing*, and in the case of man this is the Yang essence that is semen. And the more *Jing*, potentially the more *Shen* or spiritual essence.

There is a fundamental difference between Chinese and Western attitudes to sex. Traditional Chinese society was not, and is not Christian: put crudely, the more powerful or virtuous you were, the more concubines you had. So the emperor, being the Son of Heaven, had more concubines than anyone else – a noble tradition continued in our own time by Mao Tse-tung, the Great Helmsman. Furthermore, running through the gamut of sexual practices, at various times in Chinese history male and female bisexuality was looked upon tolerantly, and several of the Han emperors had infamous catamites. In male homosexual intercourse there is theoretically an exchange of Yang essence and no net loss, while women have an unlimited supply of Yin essence. Oral intercourse was looked upon favourably, as both methods enabled the man to absorb the woman's Yin secretions. Sapphism was also acceptable, and often unavoidable in a house full of young women. Indeed, when I was in the Royal Hong Kong Police there was more than one proselytizing lesbian in the force.

Many officials and wealthy merchants had a number of concubines as well as a principal wife. From personal experience I know how difficult it can be to keep one woman happy, so it is far from surprising that the Chinese developed a plethora of sexual training methods and aids. At least as far as men are concerned, these can be divided into three main types: first, those exercises such as Taoist *Baduanjin* or Eight Pieces of Brocade, by working on the circulation and the nervous system, and in particular by massaging the kidneys and the lower abdomen, enhance the

Fig 81   Sifu Lee Chun-sing performing the Baduanjin exercise Support The Sky.

functions of the urogenital system and can help with certain types of impotence. Second, there are exercises which use breath control and alternate tension and relaxing of the lower body, in particular the sphincter, to stimulate the production of internal secretions and to enable the practitioner to develop greater control and thus prolong the sexual act. Similar exercises are performed in conjunction with martial movements in a variety of Chinese martial arts, including Tai Chi Chuan.

Third, there is what the late sinologist Robert Van Gulik called 'coitus reserva-tus', the ability of a man to come to orgasm during sexual intercourse, but without emitting semen. Sexual manuals dealing with this and other matters date back to at least the Han dynasty (202 BC–220 AD), often giving advice in the form of dialogues between the legendary Yellow Emperor and the 'Dark Girl' who acts as his teacher. Much is made of the transfer of religious, philosophical and martial knowledge from India to China, yet few realize that many of the sexual practices of Tantric yoga arise out of earlier Taoist practices, including coitus reservatus.

The belief was that man's Yang essence, his Jing, was limited in quantity, whereas woman had an inexhaustible supply of Yin essence. Thus man's Yang essence had to be maximized so that he could do his duty to his ancestors by continuing the family line. To accomplish this it was essential to cohabit frequently with numerous (preferably young) female partners without emitting semen, strengthening his Yang by absorbing their Yin. Then with his Yang essence at a maximum he could have successful intercourse with the principal wife, ideally five days after the menstrual period when her Yin essence was at a maximum, and produce male offspring. By blocking the seminal duct, the theory was that, instead of letting valuable Jing escape to enter and nourish the female body, the male adept would cause it to return, go up the spinal column to nourish the brain thus transforming sexual essence into spiritual essence.

Certain Taoist monasteries and nunneries were infamous at various times in Chinese history because of the activities of both inmates and visitors. For example, the Taoist patriarch, Chang Chueh, led a mystical sect known as the

Yellow Turbans, which by 184 AD occupied large tracts of China. Their rebellion, though unsuccessful, led to the destruction of the Han dynasty. If we are to believe their Buddhist enemies, their mystic Yellow Book advocated sexual intercourse as a method of achieving the True Way, and mass sexual orgies with numerous couplings – the so-called 'four eyes and four tongues' – took place in Taoist monasteries and nunneries.

Many Chinese restaurants have statues or pictures of three Chinese gentlemen, the Gods of Prosperity, Happiness and Longevity. They each have their particular symbols and characteristics, but the God of Longevity has a massive, bulging forehead; it is said to be full of *Shen* (spiritual essence) as a result of *Jing* travelling up the spine and transforming. Unfortunately this meant that while his forehead was disproportionately large, other areas were disproportionately small.

Since the 1960s, these methods have had something of a resurgence, particularly in the west in a movement led by a number of prominent *Qi Gong* teachers – and yet none of the gentlemen teaching these methods boasts of his lack of endowment or appears to have the bulging forehead of the God of Longevity. Maybe they're not doing it right. This brings me to the lessons to be learned from a Tai Chi elder brother of mine in Hong Kong. His wife took him along to see my teacher because he was ejaculating uncontrollably in the street and at business meetings; he felt that his *Qi* was stuck and couldn't go up or down, and sometimes he even felt that he could fly. He admitted that he had trained in a sexual *Qi Gong* method with a teacher from China. My teacher was able to cure him over two days.

This kind of condition is what the Chinese term 'Walk fire, enter demon', where, as a result of incorrect teaching, incorrect or excessive practice, or as a result of combining inappropriate methods of exercise ('walk fire'), the practitioner experiences certain side effects ('enter demon'); these can range from headaches, to hallucinations, to impotence, to death. I referred earlier to certain texts published by Wu Jian-chuan's descendants in 1980: three of these, attributed to Chang San-feng and referring to internal alchemy, are clearly from this controversial tradition. I believe these texts to be spurious, and suspect that they were written by one of Yang Lu-chan's or Ban-hou's students in the imperial Court to curry favour with Manchu nobles or eunuchs who indulged in deviant practices.

Internal Alchemy for Women

So far we have considered men for the most part, but sex manuals published at various periods from the Han dynasty onwards taught methods of regulating the menstrual cycle, making it of shorter duration, more regular, and with longer periods of time between cycles. The texts also taught methods of trying to make pregnancy safer and more certain. And during the Tang dynasty, in the capital of Chang-an (now called Xian), there was a well established brothel quarter populated by volunteer, kidnapped and purchased women, registered according to their rank and trained in skills. Some high-level courtesans became noted poets and had a position of social prestige similar to that of the geisha.

Although training for women in these special physical skills is rare nowadays, it still exists in South-East Asia. Such skills are also common in ladies with a high level of ability in either yoga or Chinese martial arts. In the case of the latter, this is a by-product and not the main aim of the training, whereas in yoga there is the Tantric influence which was itself based on earlier Taoist practices.

In Tai Chi Chuan training there are some aspects of special relevance to women. First, women are taught everything the male student is taught – although in the case of *Nei Kung*, some ladies need to cease practice several days before their period begins and not resume until several days after it ends; others, on the other hand, are able to train through the period. The reason for ceasing practice is because the exercises can make the menstrual flow heavier than normal and therefore more unpleasant, rather than because of any health risk. To this day, light *Nei Kung* practice is recommended for pregnant women, although this should be done under appropriate supervision, initially at least.

Conclusion

One continuing theme throughout Chinese sexual history is that sex is not a recreational activity in the way that *Playboy* and *Cosmopolitan* magazines would have us believe, but a fundamental method of fulfilling our duty to society, a duty that has resulted in massive overpopulation, in wars of expansion, in mass poverty and starvation. Personally I don't accept all the Chinese ideas discussed here – I haven't acquired a catamite, for example – but over the centuries their approach has had one overwhelming success: 1.2 billion Chinese, and counting. So maybe it's best to uphold the view that staying with the right partner can be a way of enlightenment.

DIM MAK: THE DEATH TOUCH

As well as being used for health purposes, internal alchemy ideas also had a martial significance with the concept of vital points. Over the centuries a large body of literature has built up recommending striking certain points at specific times of the day: this is commonly known as *Dim Mak*. Liu's Chinese–English dictionary defines *Dim Mak* (*Dian Xue* in Mandarin) as 'hitting at selected points of the body, capable of causing internal bleeding and unconsciousness'. *Dim/Dian* means 'a/to point/ dot'. *Mak/Xue* means 'a hole'/'vital point' or 'to bore a hole'.

So for a technique to be *Dim Mak*, is it enough that it causes internal bleeding or unconsciousness? Many books on *Dim Mak* refer to acupuncture points and purport to show the author hitting these points with finger strikes. So to apply *Dim Mak*, do we have to know acupuncture? And should it be applied through finger strikes? Teachers of *Dim Mak* often show their skills in a completely static situation: they simply hit a stationary opponent on the right points, and down he goes. However, applying *Dim Mak* in a real situation is something else. The opponent is not stationary, many points are hidden and protected by his clothing, and you, the *Dim Mak* master, are under pressure, having to fend off his attacks as well as having to locate and strike the points appropriate to the level of violence used against you. If you make a mistake, the death touch could result in life – for you.

Ilpo Jalamo, 6th Dan in Yuishinkai

karate from Finland, has some interesting ideas of his own on *Dim Mak*. He told me of one occasion when he was sparring with a strong opponent who was able with little difficulty to absorb his reverse punches to the ribs. Ilpo then changed the configuration of his knuckles so that one knuckle protruded, making a 'phoenix-eye fist'. Again he hit the opponent with a reverse punch; and the opponent went down.

Every Chinese martial art has techniques where force is concentrated in a very small point which is then used to strike the opponent, as in the *Biu Ji* or Thrusting Fingers form in Wing Chun. In Tai Chi Chuan we also have examples of this, in the form, for example White Snake Spits Out Its Tongue, Box the Ears; in the weapons, as in Pierce the Heart, and Dot Red Between the Eyes; and in the *Nei Kung* – Leading a Goat Smoothly and Giant Python Turning Its Body. Some techniques are designed to respond to an opponent's attack by redirecting his force so as to expose his opponent's vital points to a counter.

I can well remember the martial arts press in 1987 on the subject of the world's greatest streetfighter, the only man in the world to have been taught the secret Wing Chun footwork, and of course *Dim Mak*. He was doing very nicely, making a lot of money, when he was attacked at a seminar in Cologne by a challenger from one of the other factions. So what do you think he did, the world's greatest streetfighter, the only man in the world to know *Wing Chun's* secret footwork and *Dim Mak*? He skilfully allowed himself to be swept to the floor and then proceeded to bang his face against the *Zhou Liao* pressure point on his opponent's elbow.

Some masters of *Dim Mak* publish tables giving its effect on different pressure points. Well, maybe. Under laboratory conditions, no doubt they would find their techniques most effective. But were they to try the same techniques against top level Chinese martial artists, they might not be quite so effective. As for knowledge of acupuncture points and learning Chinese – well, most people I've come across have difficulty telling left from right and speaking or writing English; and I would never let them insert needles into my perfectly formed body!

Most *Dim Mak* techniques need to be applied at fairly close quarters, and all need to be accurate. This means it is important to acquire close-quarter skills, such as those trained in pushing hands. It also means that the average martial artist will lack the skill and accuracy to use *Dim Mak* effectively. It should not be attempted except after competent instruction, and even then with the utmost care.

Dim Mak can be used in short- or long-range striking of an opponent's anatomy, either to render him incapable of offering further resistance, or to set up another technique. It can be used in locking, gripping or twisting with a view either to rendering him incapable of offering further resistance, or to set up another technique. It can be used in closing or gripping pulses, veins and arteries, temporarily or permanently.

Dim Mak, or the idea of *Dim Mak*, is something that Tai Chi Chuan practitioners should be aware of, but rather than spending their hard-earned money buying, and valuable time watching or reading *Dim Mak* tapes and books, they'd be much better off training their skills to the extent that no matter where they hit or gripped or twisted, they hurt the opponent. Unfortunately too many people want a short cut.

If you really want to test the efficacy of *Dim Mak*, you could do the same as two Scandinavian gentlemen of my acquaintance who are gradually testing every point on one another. So far they've worked out that it hurts to get hit on the nose. Dim, or what ?

11 Terminology and Jargon

One of the most intimidating aspects of Tai Chi Chuan is the use of a bewildering variety of specialized vocabulary and terms, and it is important to look at this aspect of the art.

'Terminology' simply means the names or special terms used in our area of study. 'Jargon' originally meant 'the chattering noises of small animals', and by extension, 'gibberish'. More usually, 'jargon' refers to the idioms and special vocabulary used by a particular group or profession. It is not uncommon for such jargon to be both obscure and pretentious.

MARTIAL ARTS TERMINOLOGY

As the martial arts have evolved and developed, so has the terminology and jargon used. Within the terminology of Tai Chi Chuan there are many references to animals, and it is often said that many of the techniques in Chinese martial arts in general, and Tai Chi Chuan in particular, are based on animal movements. This is not necessarily the case, however, even when techniques have names such as White Crane Flaps Its Wings or Golden Cockerel Stands on One Leg.

Whilst observing animal behaviour is likely to have played a part in the devel-opment of the art, I do believe that in many cases the names given to techniques are simply descriptive of the actions performed. Sometimes the names used contain literary allusions, sometimes even jokes. For example in *Tai Chi Nei Kung* there is the technique called Wu Gang Cutting Laurels. This unfortunate gentle-man was banished to the moon after offending the gods and was sentenced to chop the cassia trees which grow in abun-dance there – but unfortunately every mark his axe made in the tree instantly healed up. The *Nei Kung* technique not surprisingly uses repeated chopping movements.

In the sabre form there is the technique Taking off the Boots while Drunk. This refers to an incident involving the Li Bai, who was renowned for his drinking, his swordsmanship and his poetry, though not necessarily in that order. After a degree of imbibing, Li ordered the power-ful eunuch, Gao Li-shi, to take off his boots for him, thus incurring Gao's undying hatred.

The technique of Embracing the Moon exists in both Tai Chi sword and sabre forms. Our old friend, Li Bai, is said to have met his death in 761 AD when, drunk and overcome by the beauty of the reflection of the moon on the Yangtze, he

167

Fig 82   The author Embracing The Moon in Ireland.

reached out to embrace it and fell in and drowned. Incidentally the name also indicates that when applying this technique we should be leaning well forwards, rather than standing erect. In the Tai Chi spear form there is the technique called the Black-eared Kite Flies and The Fish Leaps. This is a direct quotation from the Book of Odes, most of which dates from the early Zhou dynasty that is, from around 1,000 BC.

Even 'straightforward' names such as Brush Knee Twist Step and Fist Under Elbow – or more literally, Under Elbow Look At Fist – are widely misunderstood. Many people think that Brush Knee Twist Step refers to brushing your *own* knee and twisting your *own* step, whereas the name in fact refers to diverting a kick and destroying the opponent's balance with a palm strike. Likewise, because we place the fist under the elbow when performing the eponymous technique, many believe that this is the derivation of the name, whereas in fact it derives from an upward

diversion of the opponent's punch followed by a counter punch under his elbow. Other names such as Cloud Hands are Chinese puns. The character for 'cloud' sounds similar to the character for 'turning', hence the name. The real name should be Turning Hands.

Some terminology and jargon is of more recent origin, used to refer to techniques for which the teacher doesn't know the correct name, or to techniques which he has introduced to Tai Chi Chuan from some other system. For example, one of my teacher's former students in Australia taught a technique called Willow Tree, which in fact does not exist in Tai Chi Chuan – having forgotten some of the *Nei Kung* exercises, he made some up, incorporating techniques from Wing Chun. My teacher's uncle went even further. Never a man to say 'no' to his students, he would tell them that Tai Chi had everything other systems had, including techniques such as Kuan Gung Stroking His Beard – and he even changed his form to include such techniques. Even worse, some more specialized techniques such as Running Thunder Hand he deliberately taught wrongly to certain students, one of whom, in Malaysia, was stunned in 1981 when I corrected what he had been practising wrongly for more that twenty years.

While even fifty years ago most of this nomenclature was probably not very well understood, nowadays it has become archaic, and it will remain so unless Tai Chi instructors and students spend some time researching and attempting to understand and explain their art, instead of seeking to make it more mysterious than it really is. It is for this reason that in seminars I tell the students to recite the names of the techniques as we do them in the forms.

MARTIAL ARTS JARGON

Martial artists have their own arcane and bizarre language, which has various dialects depending on the art practised. In its defence, jargon is concise and serves as a sort of shorthand in a conversation between experts; and it means that those engaged in theoretical and technical discussions understand each other immediately.

Jargon has a further morale-raising and supportive role, enabling one freemason in the Grand Lodge of Internal Martial Arts to recognize another without having to don an apron and roll up the left trouser leg. For some of us indeed, jargon also serves to evoke a measure of respect from our students, and other schools in particular, and the public in general, and also to convince them of our possession of recondite knowledge.

The two so-called 'secret sounds' of *Heng* and *Ha* are a good example of this. Supposedly Yang Lu-chan heard students of his teacher, Chen Chang-xing, emitting these secret sounds and thus learned their secret breathing method. In fact as students of Chinese mythology will know, Heng and Ha are the onomatopoeic names of a pair of Zhou dynasty (c1122BC) marshals: Cheng Lung, also known as 'Heng' meaning, literally, 'to snort'; and Chen Chi, also known as 'Ha', meaning 'to blow'. Heng could emit two columns of white light from his nostrils which consumed his enemies, while Ha could emit yellow gas which killed all those who came in contact with it. To base breathing methods on these mythical beings is as logical as to base them on the huffing and puffing used by the Big Bad Wolf to blow the Three Little Pigs' houses down.

Of course, every field of human endeavour has its own special vocabulary and technical language shouldn't automatically be considered jargon. And when, as exponents of the internal martial arts, we communicate with one another, it isn't necessarily wrong to write or speak in a way that the man in the street can't understand. The key test for jargon is whether or not the thoughts expressed could have been conveyed more simply without any loss of comprehension.

In the context of the internal martial arts, we have the further problem that many practitioners are ignorant of the terminology, while others often don't know how to use it correctly. For example, '...sexual energy is *Qi* [*Chi*]; '*Qi* is an invaluable aid in self defence'; and, 'each of the Tai Chi weapons will teach the practitioner some unique facet of extending his *Qi*'. Possibly the American Tai Chi expert who is responsible for these utterances knows more Tai Chi jargon than the term '*Qi*' – but then again, perhaps he doesn't.

One Western Tai Chi instructor has invented a plethora of lacklustre and sadly uninformative terms such as the dreaded 'Dragon Prawn' or *Lung Xia* (the Chinese term for 'lobster') – presumably it gives the opponent indigestion. Another has used the terms 'ground vectors' and '*Peng*' to describe certain types of static body mechanics, a meaning quite at variance with the very concept of *Peng Jin*. Even someone with a good command of Chinese such as Professor Douglas Wile can create problems for readers who do not read Chinese when he translates *Jin* in one place as 'energy' and at another as 'power'; and at yet another, *Nei Kung* also becomes 'inner energy'.

It is not only in the West that this

problem exists. Gu Liu-xin, one of China's foremost martial arts writers on Chen-style Tai Chi Chuan in his book *Tai Chi Chuan Shu* (*The Art of Tai Chi Chuan*) uses jargon in a way that detracts from, rather than enhances our understanding. For instance, one of my Chinese lady students asked me what Gu meant by the term '*Ning Jin*'. '*Ning*' can be found in one of my martial arts dictionaries, but not '*Ning Jin*'. The literal translation for '*Ning*' is 'to twist', and it was obvious from the context that Gu meant the use of '*Lie Jin*' which is a 'twisting' or 'spiralling force'.

When I was studying for my law degree back in Glasgow in the early seventies, one of the first things we were taught was that words take their character and colour from those that surround them. This is no less the case with Chinese characters, and sometimes the same character is used in different ways within the same paragraph or even within the same sentence. A perusal of the five major essays that constitute the Tai Chi Chuan classics – *The Theory of Tai Chi Chuan*, *The Classic of Tai Chi Chuan*, *An Exposition of the Thirteen Tactics*, *The Song Of The Thirteen Tactics* and *The Fighters Song* – reveals that while the term *Qi* is sometimes used to refer to the breath alone, and on other occasions to the circulation, in no instance is it used to mean any kind of force or power: for this, the term *Jin/Jing* is used.

In Tai Chi Chuan there are eight fundamental methods of using *Jin*, each of which is identified with one of the Eight Trigrams. I find that this is one example where the Chinese terms are much more precise than the unsatisfactory translations that exist for them in English. However, as some of these terms such as '*lu*', cannot be found in any encyclopedia or dictionary save recent ones that deal only with the martial arts, we have the possibility that either they have been deliberately invented to describe a particular action, or they were wrongly transcribed, or there was a problem with dialect.

Very often the jargon pedants and armchair warriors of Tai Chi Chuan wish to lecture us on how to use these eight methods to fight. In fact it really doesn't matter *what* techniques are used, whether in competition or real fighting; what *does* matter is that they should be effective. Criticism can be acceptable and even valuable, but only where it springs from extensive personal experience and practice.

Many of the brotherhood of the martial arts are in the 'high risk' category when it comes to the use of jargon. There are those who are insecure and who feel they must use it to make an uncaring world believe that it needs their rather dubious services. There are others who are ashamed of their own lack of knowledge and ability, and who are therefore driven to find suitable language to mask their shortcomings. And there are the aspiring elitists and would-be mystics who try and set themselves apart from the common herd by reciting an arcane litany of 'Reeling Silk energy' and '*Qi* pulses'.

It is also important to consider the marketing concept of strategic semantics. This is the art of conveying meanings which contribute to the selling effectiveness of an advertisement, and of avoiding any meanings which detract from this. There is a strong link between the use of strategic semantics and jargon, and this has led many of those martial artists who have a certain degree of genuine knowledge and ability, to bastardize and emasculate their art so that it fits the marketing image which they have created. Over the years there have been advertisements from various instructors deploying strategic semantics; so we learn that Tai Chi Chuan is 'an unexcelled but non-violent form of self defence'; 'a dance of equality'; 'strength through gentleness'; with 'continuous yielding pushing hands'.

This delightful illusion of joyful people performing their gentle art of Tai Chi in a land of milk and honey does not accord with the recent history of Tai Chi Chuan, and there would be serious consternation if this paradise were to be visited by the shades of the great masters of the past – men such as Yang Lu-chan, chief combat instructor of the Manchu Imperial Guard; or Wang Lan-ting who, after killing a number of Manchus, had to seek sanctuary in a Buddhist temple. The reality is that there are many Tai Chi practitioners who would prefer to continue to practise their 'dance of equality' than to learn the genuine art from such men.

In the recent past, the great masters were not mystic sages; many of them were not good men by either Christian or Chinese standards, and in some cases couldn't even write their own names. And yet many of them employed strategic semantics: when the Ching dynasty was overthrown at the turn of the century, the old order was destroyed and with it the position occupied in it by masters of the martial arts, and so these masters had to market their art to make it attractive and accessible to the rich men of their day. This is why, over the years, there has been 'small frame' Tai Chi Chuan, 'fast form' Tai Chi Chuan, 'simplified' Tai Chi Chuan, and so forth.

THE ORIGINS OF TAI CHI CHUAN TERMINOLOGY AND JARGON

The *Nei Jia Chuan* Tradition

We have seen the influence of Taoist philosophy and religion, and of internal alchemy on the jargon used in Tai Chi Chuan. We have also seen how a number of the names of techniques are cultural references. Let us now compare the terminology used in Tai Chi Chuan with that used in other internal martial arts. Many writers have talked about the effect that Yang Lu-chan and his sons had on the martial arts community in Beijing, but few writers have considered the impact on Yang and his descendants of that community.

First, let us look at the theory and nomenclature of *Ba Gua Zhang* and *Xing Yi Chuan*, the other two famous arts which today are referred to as *Nei Jia Chuan* or internal martial arts, and compare this to the theory and nomenclature of Tai Chi Chuan.Both *Ba Gua Zhang* and *Xing Yi* have classical writings elucidating the theory, many of which are written in mnemonic style like the Tai Chi Chuan classics. For example in *Xing Yi* there are songs of Tai Chi, Wu Chi, Seven Stars, Five Elements, and so on. And in *Ba Gua Zhang* songs there are references to The Opening and Closing Method, Suspended Headtop, Sinking the *Qi* to the *Tan Tien*, besides others.

In the names of techniques there are also similarities to Tai Chi names. So in *Ba Gua Zhang* and in Tai Chi Chuan we have the following: Retrieving The Moon from the Sea, Green Dragon Displays its Claws, White Snake Spits Out its Tongue, Giant Python Turns its Body, Embrace the Moon, Sweeping a Thousand Soldiers

Left and Right, Rhinoceros Facing the Moon, Celestial Horse Walks the Skies, Civet Cat Catching a Rat, Golden Cockerel on One Leg, Push Open the Window to Look at the Moon, and so on and so forth. Curiously most of these names are found in Tai Chi weapon forms, and only a few in the hand form or *Nei Kung*

In *Xing Yi Chuan* and in Tai Chi Chuan we have fewer names which are the same: Seven Stars, White Crane Flaps its Wings, Tai Gong Fishing and so on. However, many of the movements in both the Five Elements fist forms and the twelve animal forms have some similarity to Tai Chi Chuan techniques, though are much more linear and without such a great distinction between soft and hard.

It is impossible to say whether all three arts drew from one common martial tradition and China's rich cultural heritage, or whether they influenced one another only in Beijing – where they most certainly did. It is also impossible to say who borrowed what from whom. Moreover, in the years since the three *Nei Jia Chuan* systems came together in Beijing, many people from other disciplines have become Tai Chi Chuan instructors and so have started to bring in unrelated and foreign jargon, such as references to 'chakras' and acupuncture points, thus making mysterious the little Tai Chi Chuan they do know. This only confuses the issue further, requiring us to study acupuncture and yoga if we are able to make anything of their contributions.

The internal martial arts have many unique qualities, but these are often obscured by the incorrect and often unnecessary use of technical language which may or may not also be jargon. It is therefore important to educate first of all ourselves, and then the general public in the correct terminology and technical terms, and unless and until this is done, the internal arts will continue to be misunderstood and misrepresented.

12 Competition Tai Chi Chuan

There are no internationally accepted, standardized rules for Tai Chi Chuan competitions except for *Wu Shu Tai Chi* which is very much a minority pursuit. However, the following rules are simplified versions of those used at the British, Danish and Dutch Open Tai Chi Chuan competitions.

PUSHING HANDS RULES

Clothing
All competitors should wear suitable sports clothing. No potentially dangerous objects may be worn or carried. Competitors should be clean, with their nails clipped and long hair tied back.

Categories
The minimum age limit is sixteen years, and written parental permission is required for those under eighteen years. Weight divisions will be determined by the organizer, and a weigh-in will be conducted on the day of the competition.

Fixed Step Pushing Hands

On the referee's instructions, contestants will come into a front stance facing one another with the same front foot on the centre line. The referee will bring their arms into contact and they will begin as soon as the referee releases his hand.

Duration will be two minutes. When the timekeeper signals half time, the contestants will stop and change feet before restarting as above. The referee will stop the contest when one or both contestants loses balance, or at his discretion. He will then restart the contest. Stoppages will not be included in the contest time. When the timekeeper signals full-time, the referee will separate the contestants and await the scorer's announcement. The referee will raise the hand of the winner, and the contestants will then leave the area.

Scoring
One point will be awarded if a contestant raises his foot from the floor or steps off balance in any direction or raises any part of the rear foot from the floor. The sole of the front foot may be raised, provided that the heel is still in contact with the floor. Two points will be awarded for a half fall, ie where a contestant touches the floor with one knee or hand. Four points will be awarded for a full fall, ie where both hands/knees/the buttocks touch the floor.

If both contestants lose their balance in the same exchange, no points will be awarded. Where a contestant is losing balance and grabs the opponent's cloth-ing, two points will be awarded to his opponent.

The scorer will award points as directed by the referee. If the scores are tied, the first to score will be the winner.

Fouls and disqualifications
If a foul is committed, the referee may at his discretion warn the culprit and award two points to the opponent, or if the foul is serious, he may disqualify the offender. Fouls include attacks to the groin, legs, head or neck; punches and kicks; spear hands; throws, sweeps, locks and trips; biting, spitting and scratching; pulling hair or clothing; putting an arm or arms around the opponent's back; disobeying the referee; and dissent and foul language.

Permitted Moves
Contestants may use *peng, lu, ji, an, cai, lie, zhou* and *kao.*

Moving Step Pushing Hands

The rules shall be the same as those given above, with certain additions. The contest area will not exceed 24ft × 24ft. Contestants will approach one another at the direction of the referee from opposite ends of the contest area, and make hand/arm contact. The contest will begin on the referee's command.

Scoring
One point will be awarded where a con-testant steps outside the area. Two points will be awarded for a half fall; four points for a full fall, and eight points where a contestant is sent flying out of the area.

Permitted Moves
Contestants may move freely within the contest area using *peng, lu, ji, an, cai, lie, zhou* and *kao,* and so on.

TAI CHI FORMS

The different categories will be decided by the organizer. Competitors must wear suitable sports clothing; they may wear sports shoes or be barefooted. A panel of three judges will award points up to a maximum of ten in respect of each of the following criteria:

Hand Forms	*Weapon Forms*
1. Correct posture	1. Correct posture
2. Correct stance	2. Correct stance
3. Distinguishing Yin and Yang	3. Distinguishing Yin and Yang
4. Intent and focus	4. Intent and focus
5. Co-ordination	5. Harmony of body and weapon
6. Smooth transition from one technique to another	6. Correct use of *Jin*
7. Balanced turning and stepping	7. Balance and agility
8. Relaxation and softness	8. Control of weapon
9. Aesthetic appearance	9. Aesthetic appearance
10. Martial spirit	10. Martial spirit

Each judge will deduct five points from a competitor's total in respect of each instance of waving a *jian* (straight sword) directly overhead, performing cartwheels, splits or somersaults. Similarly five points will be deducted for each completed ten-second period by which the competitor's

Fig 83   Chua Wee-kim in forms competition.

form exceeds the time allowed. This will normally be four minutes; however, in the case of the forty-two step hand form, the time limit will be no less than five and no more than six minutes, and points will be deducted on the same basis as before in respect of which the form takes more than six or less than five minutes to complete.

The judges will disqualify any competitor whose form shown is not a recognizable Tai Chi form. After all the contestants in a category have been assessed, the three highest scorers may be asked to perform again to decide the final placings.

CHINESE FULL CONTACT FIGHTING

There are two major formats for this type of competition which normally takes place on a raised platform measuring approximately 24ft × 24ft. Unlike a boxing ring there are no ropes. The first format is referred to as *San Shou* or *San Da*, literally meaning 'scattering hands' or 'scattering striking' and thus 'free fighting'. This is different from Tai Chi *San Shou* however, in that only certain techniques are permitted and only to certain target areas. Furthermore gloves and other safety equipment are compulsory. This format is now regulated by the International Wushu Federation from mainland China.

The second format is called *Kuo Shu* or national art and is similar to *San Shou* except that points are awarded after every three or five seconds of fighting. This format is controlled by the International Kuoshu Federation which is based in Taiwan.

It has to be said that, as in other aspects of Chinese martial arts, these competitions have been used over the years by mainland China and Taiwan for political and propaganda purposes.

San Shou Rules In Brief

Full contact to the front and side of the body and head, with punches and kicks allowed.

No attacks allowed to the groin, the throat and neck, the joints and the back.

No elbow or knee strikes allowed.

Safe throws and take-downs are allowed, but they must be completed within two seconds to count as a score.

Groin guards must be worn on the inside of trousers/shorts.

No hand bandages may be worn.

There are three two-minute rounds, with one-minute intervals in between.

All contestants must be over eighteen years of age.

A valid martial arts licence must be produced on the day of the tournament.

Gum shields, groin protectors, shin and instep guards, head guards and gloves must be worn.

Points are awarded for knocking or throwing the opponent to the ground, forcing the opponent from the fighting area, and for effective punches and kicks to permissible target areas.

WU SHU TAI CHI CHUAN

The competitors perform the forty-two step combined hand form, or the combined sword form. These forms were created by putting together techniques from different Tai Chi styles; they were specifically designed for competitions held under the auspices of the International Wushu Federation which is controlled by China.

The rules for this type of competition are much more detailed; they involve deducting fractions of points for technical imperfections, such as the fingers being more than a finger's width apart when applying palm techniques. Judging such events is also highly technical, requiring the would-be officials to attend special training courses organized by the International Wushu Federation.

Because the rules are so detailed there is little point in reproducing them here. In Britain this type of competition is regulated by the British Council for Chinese Martial Arts.

THE VALUE OF COMPETITIONS

Tai Chi Chuan competitions attract a great deal of criticism: some even go so far as to say that they contravene the very philosophy of Tai Chi Chuan, though this is to misunderstand the philosophy. Thus when Chuang Tzu told his story of the legendary Peng bird which was ridiculed by small birds and cicadas for flying at vast heights all the way to the Southern Ocean on its migration, he was emphasizing the importance of acting in accordance with one's own nature. Pengs should behave like Pengs.

Competition is very popular with younger Tai Chi practitioners as it gives them the opportunity to test their skills against other martial arts in full contact competitions, and against other Tai Chi styles in the form of pushing hands. In forms competitions, young and old, male and female competitors can compete and compare their forms. I have seen forms competitors as young as seven and as old as sixty plus.

For the spectator there is the opportunity to meet other practitioners and to learn more about their own style and form by watching others. For the teachers there is the incentive to show their abilities by producing top quality competitors.

13 Postscript

In the end, Tai Chi Chuan is not about styles or schools but about the people who practise it, their personalities and their intelligence, their education and physicality, and their experiences and environment. In all this there is the eternal duality of the Yin and the Yang. In looking at the masters and the teachers, and in looking at ourselves, let us do so through the Yin/Yang microscope with which Chinese philosophy has provided us.

INNER AND OUTER, SAGE OR KING

This concept of duality pervades both Chinese philosophy and Tai Chi Chuan: there can be no inner if there is no outer, and vice versa, though it is not always clear which is which. Many Chinese schools of philosophy aimed at creating 'inner sages and outer kings'. The former implied someone such as Confucius or Lao Tzu, who had achieved moral perfection, but who could only pass on his doctrines by teaching others through his writings and discourses; often this was as a result of failing to achieve, or not wanting an official post. The latter referred to a 'doer' such as the First Emperor or Mao Tse-tung who achieved great things in the material world. The Chinese also had 'sage kings' such as King Wen, who were reputed to be philosophers and inventors.

In the historical section you saw that both 'inner sages and outer kings' have had their parts to play in the transmission of the art of Tai Chi Chuan through the ages. I will leave it to the reader to decide which masters merit which encomium.

WEN WU: CIVIL AND MARTIAL ARTS

Han Fei Tzu said 'scholars use their writings (*Wen*) to destabilize the law, while knights-errant use martial skills (*Wu*) to overthrow restrictions.' Chinese society has a long tradition of literary and other civil arts, known as *Wen*, and of martial or military pursuits, *Wu*. In religious Taoism for example, there are distinct ritual methods for the *Wen* and the *Wu* ministries. This was not, however, always the complete division of function that is sometimes thought. Many famous knight-errants were also scholars, such as the poet Li Bai, while the famous philosopher Huang Zong-xi was also a practitioner of *Nei Jia Chuan* (internal family boxing).

In Tai Chi Chuan there is a similar tradition, so Wu Yu-xiang is primarily known as an expert on Tai Chi Chuan theory, while Yang Ban-hou is primarily known as a fighter, while others such as my own teacher have been effective fighters as well as writers on the theory. However, most Tai Chi Chuan teachers do not reach a high level in either activity, the Chinese government by tradition preferring this state of affairs. In the art itself, the softer or Yin aspects are mainly designed to refine the mind intellectually and spiritually by educating the body in posture, co-ordination and respiration, thus enhancing the circulation and the nervous system. The more physically demanding or Yang aspects are designed to build a strong intent and focus, and the capacity to defend oneself accurately and effectively with body or weapons.

The true heirs to the Tai Chi tradition should be part scholar, part knight-errant – a balance of *Wen* and *Wu*. Most of us can only aspire to this ideal.

HEAVEN, EARTH AND HUMANITY

The Taoists had the concept of the three entities of heaven (supreme Yang), earth (supreme Yin) and humanity (Yin and Yang in balance) in harmony as being the Tao made manifest. Likewise on the sacred Taoist enclave of Wudang Mountain there are three heaven doors or gateways. Each seems to be the top, but after passing through the traveller realizes a long climb lies ahead. From this is derived the three doors of Tai Chi Nei Kung.

The first door is of 'inner and outer in unity', where the breath and movements are one. The second door is 'mind and body in unity' where the intent directs every action. The third door is 'heaven and thought in unity', where the physical self is forgotten though its existence continues in the real world. This is beyond technique. Someone who reaches this stage may justifiably be considered a Grand Master.

WHERE CAN I LEARN TAI CHI CHUAN?

The best way to find a Tai Chi Chuan instructor would be to contact the secretary of the Tai Chi Union for Great Britain or the British Council for Chinese Martial Arts, both of which are responsible bodies. You can write to either, enclosing a stamp addressed envelope, at the following addresses:

The Secretary TCUGB
69 Kilpatrick Gardens
Clarkston
Glasgow G76 7RF

BCCMA
9 Ashfield Road
London N14 7LA

CHART I. DIRECT CHEN FAMILY (PAO CHUI) LINEAGE

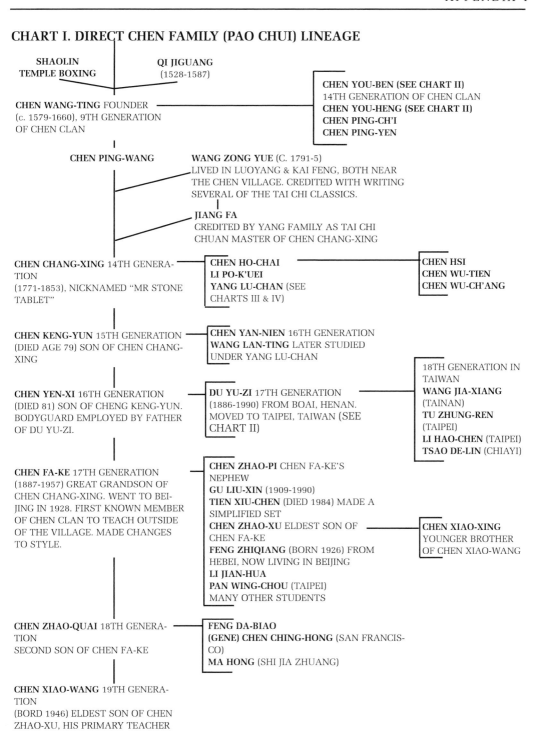

SHAOLIN
TEMPLE BOXING

QI JIGUANG
(1528-1587)

CHEN YOU-BEN (SEE CHART II)
14TH GENERATION OF CHEN CLAN
CHEN YOU-HENG (SEE CHART II)
CHEN PING-CH'I
CHEN PING-YEN

CHEN WANG-TING FOUNDER
(c. 1579-1660), 9TH GENERATION
OF CHEN CLAN

CHEN PING-WANG

WANG ZONG YUE (C. 1791-5)
LIVED IN LUOYANG & KAI FENG, BOTH NEAR
THE CHEN VILLAGE. CREDITED WITH WRITING
SEVERAL OF THE TAI CHI CLASSICS.

JIANG FA
CREDITED BY YANG FAMILY AS TAI CHI
CHUAN MASTER OF CHEN CHANG-XING

CHEN CHANG-XING 14TH GENERA-
TION
(1771-1853), NICKNAMED "MR STONE
TABLET"

CHEN HO-CHAI
LI PO-K'UEI
YANG LU-CHAN (SEE
CHARTS III & IV)

CHEN HSI
CHEN WU-TIEN
CHEN WU-CH'ANG

CHEN KENG-YUN 15TH GENERATION
(DIED AGE 79) SON OF CHEN CHANG-
XING

CHEN YAN-NIEN 16TH GENERATION
WANG LAN-TING LATER STUDIED
UNDER YANG LU-CHAN

18TH GENERATION IN
TAIWAN
WANG JIA-XIANG
(TAINAN)
TU ZHUNG-REN
(TAIPEI)
LI HAO-CHEN (TAIPEI)
TSAO DE-LIN (CHIAYI)

CHEN YEN-XI 16TH GENERATION
(DIED 81) SON OF CHENG KENG-YUN.
BODYGUARD EMPLOYED BY FATHER
OF DU YU-ZI.

DU YU-ZI 17TH GENERATION
(1886-1990) FROM BOAI, HENAN.
MOVED TO TAIPEI, TAIWAN (SEE
CHART II)

CHEN FA-KE 17TH GENERATION
(1887-1957) GREAT GRANDSON OF
CHEN CHANG-XING. WENT TO BEI-
JING IN 1928. FIRST KNOWN MEMBER
OF CHEN CLAN TO TEACH OUTSIDE
OF THE VILLAGE. MADE CHANGES
TO STYLE.

CHEN ZHAO-PI CHEN FA-KE'S
NEPHEW
GU LIU-XIN (1909-1990)
TIEN XIU-CHEN (DIED 1984) MADE A
SIMPLIFIED SET
CHEN ZHAO-XU ELDEST SON OF
CHEN FA-KE
FENG ZHIQIANG (BORN 1926) FROM
HEBEI, NOW LIVING IN BEIJING
LI JIAN-HUA
PAN WING-CHOU (TAIPEI)
MANY OTHER STUDENTS

CHEN XIAO-XING
YOUNGER BROTHER
OF CHEN XIAO-WANG

CHEN ZHAO-QUAI 18TH GENERA-
TION
SECOND SON OF CHEN FA-KE

FENG DA-BIAO
(GENE) CHEN CHING-HONG (SAN FRANCIS-
CO)
MA HONG (SHI JIA ZHUANG)

CHEN XIAO-WANG 19TH GENERA-
TION
(BORD 1946) ELDEST SON OF CHEN
ZHAO-XU, HIS PRIMARY TEACHER

CHART II. OTHER LINEAGES FROM THE CHEN CLAN

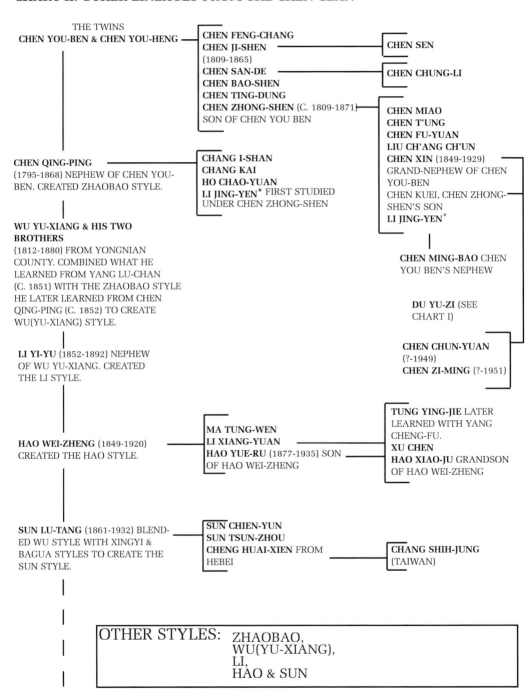

THE TWINS
CHEN YOU-BEN & CHEN YOU-HENG

CHEN FENG-CHANG
CHEN JI-SHEN
(1809-1865)
CHEN SAN-DE
CHEN BAO-SHEN
CHEN TING-DUNG
CHEN ZHONG-SHEN (C. 1809-1871)
SON OF CHEN YOU BEN

CHEN SEN

CHEN CHUNG-LI

CHEN MIAO
CHEN T'UNG
CHEN FU-YUAN
LIU CH'ANG CH'UN
CHEN XIN (1849-1929)
GRAND-NEPHEW OF CHEN
YOU-BEN
CHEN KUEI, CHEN ZHONG-
SHEN'S SON
LI JING-YEN*

CHEN QING-PING
(1795-1868) NEPHEW OF CHEN YOU-
BEN. CREATED ZHAOBAO STYLE.

CHANG I-SHAN
CHANG KAI
HO CHAO-YUAN
LI JING-YEN* FIRST STUDIED
UNDER CHEN ZHONG-SHEN

**WU YU-XIANG & HIS TWO
BROTHERS**
(1812-1880) FROM YONGNIAN
COUNTY. COMBINED WHAT HE
LEARNED FROM YANG LU-CHAN
(C. 1851) WITH THE ZHAOBAO STYLE
HE LATER LEARNED FROM CHEN
QING-PING (C. 1852) TO CREATE
WU(YU-XIANG) STYLE.

CHEN MING-BAO CHEN
YOU BEN'S NEPHEW

DU YU-ZI (SEE
CHART I)

LI YI-YU (1852-1892) NEPHEW
OF WU YU-XIANG. CREATED
THE LI STYLE.

CHEN CHUN-YUAN
(?-1949)
CHEN ZI-MING (?-1951)

HAO WEI-ZHENG (1849-1920)
CREATED THE HAO STYLE.

MA TUNG-WEN
LI XIANG-YUAN
HAO YUE-RU (1877-1935) SON
OF HAO WEI-ZHENG

TUNG YING-JIE LATER
LEARNED WITH YANG
CHENG-FU.
XU CHEN
HAO XIAO-JU GRANDSON
OF HAO WEI-ZHENG

SUN LU-TANG (1861-1932) BLEND-
ED WU STYLE WITH XINGYI &
BAGUA STYLES TO CREATE THE
SUN STYLE.

SUN CHIEN-YUN
SUN TSUN-ZHOU
CHENG HUAI-XIEN FROM
HEBEI

CHANG SHIH-JUNG
(TAIWAN)

OTHER STYLES: ZHAOBAO,
WU(YU-XIANG),
LI,
HAO & SUN

CHART III. DIRECT YANG FAMILY LINEAGE

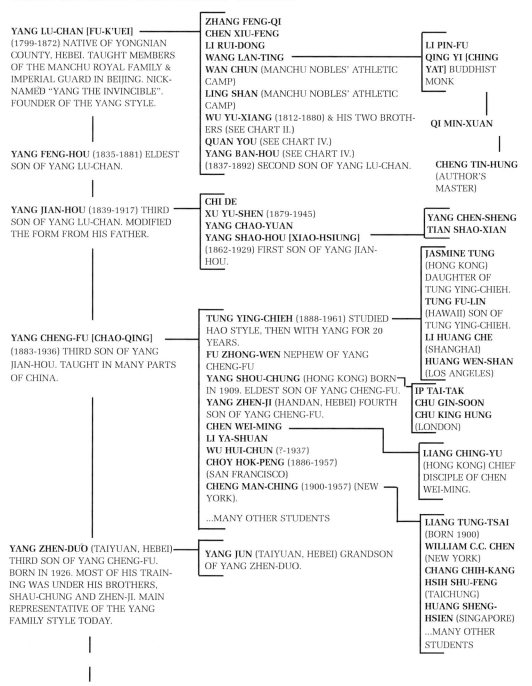

YANG LU-CHAN [FU-K'UEI] (1799-1872) NATIVE OF YONGNIAN COUNTY, HEBEI. TAUGHT MEMBERS OF THE MANCHU ROYAL FAMILY & IMPERIAL GUARD IN BEIJING. NICKNAMED "YANG THE INVINCIBLE". FOUNDER OF THE YANG STYLE.

ZHANG FENG-QI
CHEN XIU-FENG
LI RUI-DONG
WANG LAN-TING
WAN CHUN (MANCHU NOBLES' ATHLETIC CAMP)
LING SHAN (MANCHU NOBLES' ATHLETIC CAMP)
WU YU-XIANG (1812-1880) & HIS TWO BROTHERS (SEE CHART II.)
QUAN YOU (SEE CHART IV.)
YANG BAN-HOU (SEE CHART IV.) (1837-1892) SECOND SON OF YANG LU-CHAN.

LI PIN-FU
QING YI [CHING YAT] BUDDHIST MONK

QI MIN-XUAN

CHENG TIN-HUNG (AUTHOR'S MASTER)

YANG FENG-HOU (1835-1881) ELDEST SON OF YANG LU-CHAN.

YANG JIAN-HOU (1839-1917) THIRD SON OF YANG LU-CHAN. MODIFIED THE FORM FROM HIS FATHER.

CHI DE
XU YU-SHEN (1879-1945)
YANG CHAO-YUAN
YANG SHAO-HOU [XIAO-HSIUNG] (1862-1929) FIRST SON OF YANG JIAN-HOU.

YANG CHEN-SHENG
TIAN SHAO-XIAN

YANG CHENG-FU [CHAO-QING] (1883-1936) THIRD SON OF YANG JIAN-HOU. TAUGHT IN MANY PARTS OF CHINA.

TUNG YING-CHIEH (1888-1961) STUDIED HAO STYLE, THEN WITH YANG FOR 20 YEARS.
FU ZHONG-WEN NEPHEW OF YANG CHENG-FU.
YANG SHOU-CHUNG (HONG KONG) BORN IN 1909. ELDEST SON OF YANG CHENG-FU.
YANG ZHEN-JI (HANDAN, HEBEI) FOURTH SON OF YANG CHENG-FU.
CHEN WEI-MING
LI YA-SHUAN
WU HUI-CHUN (?-1937)
CHOY HOK-PENG (1886-1957) (SAN FRANCISCO)
CHENG MAN-CHING (1900-1957) (NEW YORK).

...MANY OTHER STUDENTS

JASMINE TUNG (HONG KONG) DAUGHTER OF TUNG YING-CHIEH.
TUNG FU-LIN (HAWAII) SON OF TUNG YING-CHIEH.
LI HUANG CHE (SHANGHAI)
HUANG WEN-SHAN (LOS ANGELES)

IP TAI-TAK
CHU GIN-SOON
CHU KING HUNG (LONDON)

LIANG CHING-YU (HONG KONG) CHIEF DISCIPLE OF CHEN WEI-MING.

YANG ZHEN-DUŎ (TAIYUAN, HEBEI) THIRD SON OF YANG CHENG-FU. BORN IN 1926. MOST OF HIS TRAINING WAS UNDER HIS BROTHERS, SHAU-CHUNG AND ZHEN-JI. MAIN REPRESENTATIVE OF THE YANG FAMILY STYLE TODAY.

YANG JUN (TAIYUAN, HEBEI) GRANDSON OF YANG ZHEN-DUO.

LIANG TUNG-TSAI (BORN 1900)
WILLIAM C.C. CHEN (NEW YORK)
CHANG CHIH-KANG
HSIH SHU-FENG (TAICHUNG)
HUANG SHENG-HSIEN (SINGAPORE)
...MANY OTHER STUDENTS

CHART IV. YANG & WU LINEAGES

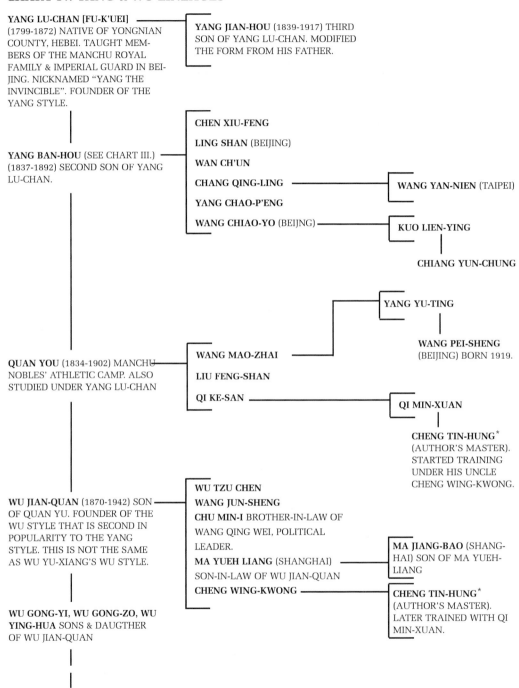

YANG LU-CHAN [FU-K'UEI] (1799-1872) NATIVE OF YONGNIAN COUNTY, HEBEI. TAUGHT MEMBERS OF THE MANCHU ROYAL FAMILY & IMPERIAL GUARD IN BEIJING. NICKNAMED "YANG THE INVINCIBLE". FOUNDER OF THE YANG STYLE.

YANG JIAN-HOU (1839-1917) THIRD SON OF YANG LU-CHAN. MODIFIED THE FORM FROM HIS FATHER.

YANG BAN-HOU (SEE CHART III.) (1837-1892) SECOND SON OF YANG LU-CHAN.

CHEN XIU-FENG

LING SHAN (BEIJING)

WAN CH'UN

CHANG QING-LING

YANG CHAO-P'ENG

WANG CHIAO-YO (BEIJNG)

WANG YAN-NIEN (TAIPEI)

KUO LIEN-YING

CHIANG YUN-CHUNG

QUAN YOU (1834-1902) MANCHU NOBLES' ATHLETIC CAMP. ALSO STUDIED UNDER YANG LU-CHAN

WANG MAO-ZHAI

LIU FENG-SHAN

QI KE-SAN

YANG YU-TING

WANG PEI-SHENG (BEIJING) BORN 1919.

QI MIN-XUAN

CHENG TIN-HUNG* (AUTHOR'S MASTER). STARTED TRAINING UNDER HIS UNCLE CHENG WING-KWONG.

WU JIAN-QUAN (1870-1942) SON OF QUAN YOU. FOUNDER OF THE WU STYLE THAT IS SECOND IN POPULARITY TO THE YANG STYLE. THIS IS NOT THE SAME AS WU YU-XIANG'S WU STYLE.

WU TZU CHEN

WANG JUN-SHENG

CHU MIN-I BROTHER-IN-LAW OF WANG QING WEI, POLITICAL LEADER.

MA YUEH LIANG (SHANGHAI) SON-IN-LAW OF WU JIAN-QUAN

CHENG WING-KWONG

MA JIANG-BAO (SHANGHAI) SON OF MA YUEH-LIANG

CHENG TIN-HUNG* (AUTHOR'S MASTER). LATER TRAINED WITH QI MIN-XUAN.

WU GONG-YI, WU GONG-ZO, WU YING-HUA SONS & DAUGTHER OF WU JIAN-QUAN

Appendix II
Chronological Table of Tai Chi Chuan

MARTIAL ARTS/EXERCISE SYSTEMS

Ritual martial arts contests using a form of wrestling during the Zhou dynasty (c.1100BC).
Mention by Lao Tzu (c.400BC) and Chuang Tzu (c.300BC) of concentrating Qi and breathing methods.
Chart showing Chinese soft calisthenics found in tomb (c.168BC) at Ma Wang Dui.
Cheng Ling-xi from Anhui learns Small Nine Heavens Boxing from Han Gong-yue during the Liang dynasty (502–557AD) and passes on the art within the Cheng family.

Xu Xuan-ping teaches 37 Styles Boxing to Song Yuan-qiao in Anhui Province.

Li Dao-zi teaches Prior to Heaven Boxing on Wudang Mountain to the Yu clan and others.
Yin Li-xiang teaches After Heaven Boxing to Hu Jing-zi and Song Zhong-shu.
Emperor Hui Zong (1101–25) said by Huang Zong-xi to have sent for Chang San-feng.
Chang San-feng said by Wu Tu-nan to have been born in 1247.
Wong Shiu-hon suggests more likely date for Chang's birth would be c.1314.
The painter Huang Gong-wang and Chang San-feng are involved with Complete Truth Taoist sect on Wudang Mountain c.1330–40.
Emperor Tai Tzu sends for Chang in 1372.
Emperor Cheng Tzu sends an expedition to search for Chang (1407-16).
Emperor Cheng Tzu sends a second expedition to search for Chang (1419-23).
Imperial tablet inscribed to Chang at the Golden Pavilion Temple in Bao Ji (1434–46).

HISTORY AND CIVILISATION

The Book of Changes (Yi Ching) used by the Zhou Emperors for the purposes of divination.
Age of the Philosophers (c.500–100BC).
221BC Unification of China under the First Emperor of Qin.
Writing of The Book of History by Grand Historian Sima Qian (c.145–86BC).
527AD Bodhidharma comes to China from India to set up the Chan (Zen) Buddhist school at the Shaolin Temple, Henan.
565 The term 'Nei Jia' (Internal Family) is used in a Buddhist text.
Li Bai (701-62), poet and knight-errant, roams China in search of sages, hermits and adventure.
General An Lu-shan's Rebellion (755-763).
770 Tu Fu, poet and friend of Li Bai, dies.
906 The Tang ends and the 5 Dynasties begin.

1108 Death of philosopher Cheng Yi of the Tai Chi Diagram Sect.
1200 Death of Neo Confucian philosopher Chu Xi.
1227 Deaths of Genghis Khan & his Taoist adviser.
1324 the Yellow River changes course.
1336 the Yellow River returns to its old course.
1368 Foundation of the Ming dynasty
1405–33 Maritime expeditions to the Persian Gulf, Red Sea and East Africa.
1421 decision to move the capital from Nanjing to Beijing.
1440–1 Construction of the palaces in Beijing.

1459 Ying Zong Emperor issues imperial decree honouring Chang San-feng.

c.1520-50 Wang Zong transmits Nei Jia Chuan to Chen Zhou-tong. In Zhejiang it is transmitted to Chang Song-xi.
General Qi Ji-guang (1528–87) writes the Chuan Ching (Classic of Boxing).
c. 1620 death of Chang Song-xi of Nei Jia Chuan.

1638 Chen Yuan-bin goes to Nagasaki where he teaches what later became Jujutsu (Soft Art).
c.1650 Chen Wang-ting from Chenjiakou, Henan Province teaches boxing.
1669 Death of Wang Zheng-nan. Huang's inscription on his gravestone mentions Nei Jia Chuan and Chang San-feng.
1728 The Yong Zheng Emperor issues a general prohibition of the martial arts.
1791 Wang Zong-yue in Luoyang, Henan Province.
1795 Wang in Kaifeng, Henan Province.
c.1800 Chen Chang-xing (1771–1853) teaches TCC in Chen village.
c.1810 Yang Lu-chan (1799–1872) arrives in the Chen village.
c.1850 Yang returns home to Yongnian.

c.1852 Yang goes to Beijing.
1852 Wu Yu-xiang goes to the Zhaobao village for a month to train with Chen Qing-ping.
1908–9 Song Shu-ming appears in Beijing with an ancient text and teaches many masters.

1469 Official Ming records show a bureaucracy of 80,000 military and over 100,000 civil officials.
1528 Death of Wang Shou-ren, founder of doctrine of 'Knowledge and Conduct in Unity'.
1598 Death of Lin Chao-en, founder of the syncretic sect of the three teachings.
1615–27 Conflict between the court eunuchs and the Confucianists of the Tunglin Academy.
1649 Huang Zong-xi and other resistance leaders go to Nagasaki seeking aid against the Manchus.
1640 Chen Wang-ting leads county soldiers to support local magistrate against traitor Liu.
1676 Publication of Ming Ru Xue An – an intellectual history of the Ming – written by the same Huang Xong-xi.
1728 Printing of an illustrated encyclopedia containing almost ten million characters.
1796 Death of philosopher/ historian Zhang Xue-cheng: The present is history; history is the Tao made manifest.
1795–1803 Rebellion of the White Lotus secret society.
1812 Census reveals 361 million inhabitants.

1842 Treaty of Nanking cedes Hong Kong to Britain and opens Chinese ports to opium.
1850 Beginning of the Taiping rebellion.
1854 The Taiping threaten Beijing
1860 French and British troops sack Beijing.

1900 The Boxers occupy Beijing and besiege the embassies.

Glossary

An – Downward directed push /press.

Baduanjin – Eight Pieces of Brocade. Chinese soft exercise for health sometimes including techniques to stimulate the reproductive system.

Ba Gua/Pa Kua – Eight Trigrams, consisting the four cardinal points and four corners.

Ba Gua Zhang – Eight Trigram Palm; internal martial art based on Eight Trigrams.

Bai Shi – Ceremony of ritual initiation.

Bao Yi – To embrace the one (i.e. the *Tao*).

Bu – Footwork and stances.

Cai – A plucking or uprooting force.

Catty – Chinese unit of measure weighing more than one pound.

Chan – School of Buddhism with heavy Chinese influences; better known in the West by its Japanese name of *Zen*.

Chang Chuan – Long Boxing. An alternative name for Tai Chi Chuan as well as the name given to a hard style boxing form.

Chi/Qi – Vital energy, including the air and breath. (N.B. not the same Chi as in Tai Chi!)

Chi Kung/Qi Gong – a method of training designed to increase the vital energy, for martial, health or meditative purposes which can be hard or soft in nature.

Chien – Trigram/hexagram representing Heaven and Supreme Yang.

Ching/Jing – Classic or Book.

Chuan/Quan – Fist. By extension a system of fighting or boxing.

Da Lu – Great sideways diversion. Popular name for famous pushing hands exercise more properly known as Four Corners or Eight Gates Five Steps.

Dan Tian/Tan Tien – Cinnabar field, area just below the navel where Chinese alchemists considered internal energy was developed.

Dao – The sabre.

Di Zi – Disciple.

Dim Mak/Dian Xue – Vital point attacks.

Fu Qi – Spirit writing, where the medium suspends a writing brush over a planchette filled with sand and then invokes a spirit who communicates by tracing characters on the sand.

Gong/Kung – Work/effort involving a degree of skill. In Chinese martial arts this usually refers to various types of conditioning training.

Hsing I/Xing Yi Chuan – Form and Intent Boxing; one of the three major internal styles.

I Ching/Yi Jing – Book/Classic of Change. A book of divination dating from before 1000 BC in one form or another.

Jeet Kune Do – Cantonese term meaning 'Direct Fist Way'. The concept of the late Bruce Lee to absorb only what was of direct use from the traditional styles.

Ji – A straight push.

Jia – Literally family or school.

Jian – Sword.

Jiao Lian – Trainer or coach.

Jin/Jing – Force. We listen for our opponent's Jin and redirect it with our own before discharging Jin at our opponent.

Jing – Vital (often seminal) essence. (N.B. not the same Jing as means force).

Kao – To lean. Applying force using the shoulder or back.

Kung Fu/Gongfu – Skill/effort/workmanship. Often used by Cantonese speakers and Westerners to refer to Chinese boxing.

Lao Shi – Old (i.e. venerable) teacher. Term of respect for teacher or master.

Li – Strength.

Lie – Using spiralling force.

Lu – Diverting an oncoming force to the side and into emptiness.

Lun – Theory/analect/discourse.

Men Ren – Door Person. One who has become a disciple of a master.

Mian Chuan – Cotton Boxing. Early name for Tai Chi Chuan.

Nei Jia Chuan – Internal Family Boxing.

Including such arts as *Tai Chi Chuan, Ba Gua Zhang* and *Xing Yi Chuan*.

Nei Dan – Internal alchemy.

Nei Kung – Internal strength. More specifically a reference to the 24 Yan and Yang Internal Strength exercises.

Pai – School of thought/boxing.

Pao Chui – Cannon punch. Name given to Chen Family boxing and to their second form.

Peng – Upwardly directed force, e.g. to divert a push upwards.

Qiang – Spear.

Rou – Soft.

San Shou – Fighting techniques. Can also refer to choreographed two person forms or to Chinese full contact fighting.

Shaolin – Referring to the Buddhist temples of that name in Henan and Fujian provinces and by extension to external martial arts identified with these temples.

Shen – Spiritual energy.

Shi San Shi – Thirteen Postures/Tactics. an old name for Tai Chi Chuan.

Shi – Style. e.g. Hao Shi – (Tai Chi Chuan) in the style of Hao.

Sifu/Shifu – Teaching father. By extension any teacher or highly skilled person.

Song – Relaxed.

Tael – Chinese unit of weight, slightly more than an ounce.

Tai Chi/Taiji – The Supreme Pole/Ultimate composed of Yin and Yang.

Tai Chi Chuan/Taijiquan – A system of martial arts and exercise based on Yin and Yang.

Tao – The Way or Ways to enlightenment or self development followed by the Taoists.

Tao Te Ching – Way and Virtue/Power Classic. Prime Taoist text credited to Lao Tzu (the Old Boy).

Tui Shou – Pushing hands. Various partnered drills and exercises designed to improve skills such as close quarter control of an opponent, evasion coordination etc. Can also refer to free or competition pushing hands, where the object is to unbalance the opponent.

Tu Di – Student or apprentice. Drugs etc.

Wu Chi/Ji – No Ultimate. State before Tai Chi.

Wudang – Referring to the mountain of that name.

Wai Dan – External alchemy. The use of medicines and by extension a reference to internal martial arts.

Wai Jia – External family referring to hard style martial arts.

Wu Shu – Martial arts. Nowadays this Mandarin term has come to be used mainly in reference to the highly acrobatic and artistic modern martial arts routines.

Yang – Active, male, positive principle representing strong, hard, external, bright, day, Heaven etc.

Yi – The intent.

Yin – Passive, female, negative principle representing gentle, soft, internal, dark, night, Earth etc.

Zhen Chuan – True Transmission from a master to a disciple.

Zhen Ren – True Person. Someone who by Taoistic methods has become a sage.

Zhong Ding – Centrally fixed corresponding to the element Earth.

Zhong Yong – Doctrine of the Mean, text of the Confucians. Philosophical concept of acting only to the degree necessary, neither more nor less.

Zhong Zheng – Centred and straight (though not necessarily upright).

Zhou – The use of the forearm or elbow in defence or offence.

Zu Shi – Founding teacher. Chang San-feng.

Bibliography

Benson Herbert, M.D. *The Relaxation Response* (William Morrow and Company, 1975)

Berlin, J. A. *The Syncretic Religion of Lin Chao-en* (Columbia University Press, 1990)

Chen Ping San *Chen Shi Tai Chi Chuan Tu Shuo* (Chen Xiang Ji Shu Ju Chu Ban) *Chen Style* (Taijiquan. Hai Feng Publishing Co, 1984)

Chen Wei Ming *Tai Chi Chuan Da Wen* (Tai Bei, Hua Lian Chu Ban She, 1981)

Cheng Tin Hung *Tai Chi Chuan Jing Jian* (Cheng Tin Hung Tai Chi Jian Shen Xue Yuan Chu Ban)

Cheng Tin Hung *Tai Chi Chuan Shu Yao* (Hong Kong Tai Chi Assosiation)

Cheng Tin Hung *Tai Chi Sabre, Sword, Spear* (Tai Chi Shan Zhuang)

de Bary, W. T. et. al. *Sources of Chinese Tradition*, Volumes 1 & 2 (Columbia University Press, 1960)

Dong Ying Jie *Tai Chi Chuan Shi Yi* (Hong Kong Hua Lian Chu Ban She)

Draeger, D. F. and Smith, R. W. *Asian Fighting Arts* (Berkeley Publishing Corporation, 1969)

Esherick, J. W. *The Origins of the Boxer Uprising* (University of California Press, 1987)

Fung Yu-lan *A History of Chinese Philosophy*, Volumes I + II (Princeton Paperback Printing, 1983)

Grandmasters Magazine (China Direct, 1991)

Gu Liu Xin *Pao Chui* (Hai Feng Chu Ban She, 1985, 1986)

Gu Liu Xin *Tai Chi Chuan Shu* (Zhong Guo Tu Shu Kan Xing She, 1985, 1986)

He Shao Ru *Wu Shi Tai Chi Chuan* (Ren Min Ti Yu Chu Ban She, 1963)

Henan Sheng Wen Xian *Chen Jia Gou Tai Chi Chuan Xue Xiao Jiang Yi* (Chen Jia Gou Wu Shu Guan, 1986)

Keown-Boyd, H. *Boxer Rebellion* (Leo Cooper, 1991)

Lau, D.C. (trans.) *Tao Te Ching* (The Chinese University Press, Hong Kong, 1963, 1982)

Legge, J. (trans.) *I Ching* (Bantam, 1969)

Liang, T. T. *Imagination Becomes Reality* (Bubbling-Well Press, 1984)

Liang, T. T. *T'ai Chi Ch'uan* (Random House, Inc, 1977)

Liao Guang Sen Bian Zhu *Nei Jia Tai Chi Chuan Da Quan* (Liao Jing Zhi Tai Ji Jian Shen Hui)

Liu, J. J.Y. *The Chinese Knight-Errant* (Routledge and Kegan Paul Ltd., 1967)

Long Zi Xiang *Tai Chi Chuan Xue* (Hong Kong Jing Hua Chu Ban She)

Ma You Qing *Tai Chi Chuan Zhi Yan Jiu* (Shang Wu Yin Shu Guan Hong Kong Fen Guan, 1984)

Ma Yue Liang, Xu Wen *Wu Shi Tai Chi Chuan Tui Shou* (Shanghai Shu Ju Youxian Gong Si Chu Ban, 1986)

Naquin (ed.) *Pilgrims and Sacred Sites in China* (The University of California Press, 1992)

Punin, Luo Gui Cheng *Tang Song Yin Yang Wu Xing Lun Ji* (Hong Kong Gong Cheng She, 1982)

Ronan and Needham *The Shorter Science & Civilization in China*, Vols. 1 + 2 (Cambridge University Press, 1978, 1981)

Saso, M. *The Teachings of Taoist Master Chuang* (Yale University Press, 1978)

Seidel, A. *Self and Society in Ming Thought* (Columbia University Press, 1970)

Smith, R. W. *Chinese Boxing: Masters and Methods* (North Atlantic Books, 1974)

Sun Lu Tang *Tai Chi Chuan Xue* (Hong Kong Wu Shu Chu Ban She)

Tseng Chiu Yien *The Chart of Tai Chi Chuan* (Union Press Ltd.)

Van Gulik, R.H. *Sexual Life in Ancient China* (Leiden E.J. Brill, 1974)

Vercammen, D. *The History of Tai Chi* (Chuan Dao Association, 1991)

Wang Hong Qi *Shan Qi De Ba Gua Wen Hua You Xi* (Nan Yue Chu Ban She, 1990)

Wang Peisheng & Zeng Weiq *Wu Style Taijiquan* (1983)

Wang Wei Shen *Wudang*

Song Xi Pai Nei Jia Quan (Hong Kong Hai Feng Chu Ban She You Xian Gong Si, 1989)

Werner, E.T.C *Myths and Legends of China* (Graham Brash, 1984)

Wile, D. *Lost T'ai-Chi Classics from the Late Ch'ing Dynasty* (State University of New York Press, 1996)

Wong Shiu Hon *Chang San-feng Ch'uan-Chi* (The Complete Works of Chang San-feng) (Australian National University Press, 1982)

Wu Gong Zao *Wu Jia Tai Chi Chuan* (Hong Kong Jian Quan She Chu Ban Xiao Zu, 1980, 1981)

Wu Tu Nan *Nei Jia Quan Tai Chi Gong Xuan Xuan Dao* (Hong Kong Jing Hua Chu Ban She)

Wu, L. *The Origin and Dissemination of Chinese Characters* (Caves Books Ltd., 1990)

Wudang (magazine)

(Wudang Bian Ji Bu, 1986,1)

Xiao Tian Shi *Nei Wai Gong Tu Shuo Ming Ji Yao* (Zi You Chu Ban She)

Xie Ting Bai *Chen Shi Tai Chi Pao Chui Quan* (Hua Lian Chu Ban She, 1982)

Yang Style, Taijiquan (Hai Feng Publishing Co, 1988)

Zhang San Feng *Chang San Feng Tai Chi Lian Ce Mi Jue* (Tai Bei Zi You Chu Ban She, 1982)

Zheng Can *Ding Zheng Yi Jing Lai Zhu Tu Jie* (Zhong Guo Kong Xue Hui, 1978)

Zheng Rong Guang *Tai Chi Chuan Hui Bian* (Wu Shu Chu Ban She)

Zhong Guo Dao Jiao (magazine) (Zhong Guo Dao Jiao Xie Hui, 1993,2)

Zhong Zi Ruo *Tai Chi Chuan Zhi Li Lun Yu Shi Yong* (Tai Bei Shi 'Zheng Zhong Shu Ju', 1975)

Index